Washington

BY THEME

DAY TRIPS

Ellie Kozlowski

Adventure Publications
Cambridge, Minnesota

Safety Note Washington State is home to a host of potentially dangerous animals including rattlesnakes, bears, and mountain lions, as well as natural hazards, such as extreme temperatures, avalanches, mudslides, bluffs and drop-offs (not to mention the possibility of volcanic activity, earthquakes, and tsunamis). Always heed posted safety warnings, take commonsense safety precautions, and remain aware of your surroundings. You're responsible for your own safety.

Editors: Brett Ortler and Amber Kaye Henderson

Cover and book design by Jonathan Norberg

Front cover photo: Mount Rainier: **Dene' Miles/shutterstock.com**; map, **Globe Turner/ shutterstock.com**

Back cover photo: Fort Nisqually, Tacoma: **Loren L. Masseth/shutterstock.com**

Interior photos by **Ellie Kozlowski** except as follows:

Pg. 58: **Mo Aristegui**; pg. 88: **Maria Palla Abad**

Photos used under license from Shutterstock.com: pg. 152: **alens**; pg. 43: **AleRa**; pg. 144: **Amehime**; pg. 113: **Mark Roger Bailey**; pg. 145 (top): **boreala**; pg. 109: **J Bradwin**; pg. 111: **Darryl Brooks**; pg. 142: **Cascades Creatives**; pg. 50: **cdrin**; pg. 129: **Checubus**; pg. 53: **Paula Cobleigh**; pg. 13: **Bob Coffen**; pg. 44: **Brandon Coy**; pg. 74: **Dan Larson Roam Studios**; pg. 80: **J Daracunas**; pg. 63: **DeshaCAM**; pg. 149 (top): **dvande**; pg. 121: **Aaron M. Farrar**; pg. 141: **GibsonDSLRUSeeingThis**; pg. 145 (bottom): **Globe Turner**; pg. 105: **HildeAnna**; pg. 147 (top): **Dec Hogan**; pg. 54, pg. 57 and pg. 146 (top): **Mariusz S. Jurgielewicz**; pg. 49: **Eugene Kalenkovich**; pg. 150 (bottom): **Tory Kallman**; pg. 136: **kgelati**; pg. 118 and pg. 135: **Roman Khomlyak**; pg. 149 (bottom): **Rich Koele**; pg. 147 (bottom): **Brian Lasenby**; pg. 40: **Joyce Marrero**; pg. 151 (top): **Virginie Merckaert**; pg. 21: **Bridget Moyer**; pg. 150 (top): **NatureDiver**; pg. 148 (bottom): **Sheldon Perry**; pg. 146 (bottom): **Photodigitaal.nl**; pg. 153: **Suzanna Pratt**; pg. 28: **William T Smith**; pg. 31: **SNC Arts and More**; pg. 151 (bottom): **South12th Photography**; pg. 14: **Patrick Tr**; pg. 94: **Warren Price Photography**; pg. 6: **Erika Weeks**; pg. 130: **WellyWelly**; pg. 70: **Owen Whiting**; pg. 64: **curtis wibe**; pg. 73: **J. Robert Williams**; pg. 27 and pg. 98: **Emily Marie Wilson**; pg. 22 and pg. 148 (top): **Nadia Yong**

10 9 8 7 6 5 4 3 2

Washington Day Trips by Theme
Copyright © 2021 by Michelle L. Kozlowski
Published by Adventure Publications
An imprint of AdventureKEEN
310 Garfield Street South
Cambridge, Minnesota 55008
(800) 678-7006
adventurepublications.net
All rights reserved
Printed in China
ISBN 978-1-59193-924-5 (pbk.); ISBN 978-1-59193-925-2 (ebook)

Disclaimer Please note that travel information changes under the impact of many factors that influence the travel industry. We therefore suggest that you call ahead for confirmation when making your travel plans. Every effort has been made to ensure the accuracy of information throughout this book, and the contents of this publication are believed to be correct at the time of printing. Nevertheless, the publishers cannot accept responsibility for errors or omissions, for changes in details given in this guide, or for the consequences of any reliance on the information provided by the same. Assessments of attractions and so forth are based upon the author's own experiences; therefore, descriptions given in this guide necessarily contain an element of subjective opinion, which may not reflect the publisher's opinion or dictate a reader's own experience on another occasion.

Table of Contents

Dedication

To the curious, the spontaneous, and those willing to go the extra mile.

Acknowledgments

Without the encouragement and support I received from my community of friends, colleagues, writers, and family, I would not have been able to write this book. Thank you all.

A giant, giant thank-you to Brett Ortler from AdventureKEEN for placing this project with me. You helped me cultivate an even greater love of Washington State (which I didn't know was possible). Amber Kaye Henderson—editor extraordinaire—thank you for your keen eye and fine-tooth comb. And thank you to Kate Johnson and Liliane Opsomer for your dedication and support.

Thank you to my fellow day-trippers: Denise Miller, Erica Chang, Rachel Toor, and Theo Pauline Nestor—it was an adventure doing research with you.

Thank you to all of you who generously offered up your favorite day trips when I inquired online, at social gatherings, and at my place of work—especially Bruce Whitmore, Naomi Whitmore, Maria Abad, Jenna Kruger Behrman, Melissa Lindstrum, Geneva Randall, Emma Vice, Emily Ballert-Dalrymple, and Cynthia Dukich. Your recommendations and insight proved invaluable.

A shout-out to my writing pals who were by my side (literally) during part of this project: Maya Jewell Zeller, Linda Cooper, Sonora Jha, Ruchika Tulshyan, Jessica C. Trupin, Novera Alim King, Anne Kilfoyle, and Aileen Keown Vaux.

Thanks to the people behind HistoryLink.org—your dedication to documenting regional history is both admirable and informative.

And a warm, magic-hour thank-you to those of you who helped with photography, including Cat Stoothoff, Maria Abad, Erica Chang, and especially Mo Aristegui.

To Sean Koenig: You are a lifesaver. Your support—and research!—buoyed me when I needed it most.

And a waterfall of thank-yous to my partner and greatest champion, Jonah Kozlowski, who is always willing to jump into glacial water and report back.

Land Acknowledgment

The trips throughout this book take place across the traditional lands of many Indigenous peoples, including the Makah, Klallam, Lower Elwha Klallam, S'Klallam, Chimakum, Quileute, Hoh, Quinault, Cowlitz, Chehalis, Kwalhioqua, Chinook, Lower Chinook, Sahaptin, Tenino, Yakama, Klickitat, Walla Walla, Wasco-Wishram, Palouse, Wanapum, Umatilla, Sinkiuse-Columbia, Columbia-Wenatchi, Nlaka'pamux, Puget Sound Salish, Duwamish, Puyallup, Muckleshoot, Snohomish, Snoqualmie, Nisqually, Suquamish, Upper Skagit, Squaxin, Swinomish, Twana, Skokomish, Samish, Stillaguamish, Sauk-Suiattle, Tulalip, Nooksack, Lummi, Halkomelem, Colville, Nespelem, Entiat, Okanagan, Methow, San Poil, Sinixt, Nez Perce, Chelan, Kalispel, Spokane, Ktunaxa/Kutenai, Salish and Kootenai, Schitsu'umsh/Couer D'Alene, and Cayuse tribes.

I am grateful to live on the traditional land of the Coast Salish People, including the Duwamish People, and I am full of gratitude when I visit and greet the lands beyond. I will be donating 50% of the royalties from this book to Indigenous-centered nonprofits and organizations, and/or directly to Washington State tribes. To learn more about which tribes' ancestral lands you are visiting on your day trip, use native-land.ca as a resource to get started. To learn more about the movement to return Indigenous lands to Indigenous people, visit landback.org.

Big Four Ice Caves (see page 3)

WASHINGTON STATE HAS INCREDIBLE DIVERSITY

when it comes to its geography and climates. In addition to boasting three national parks, Washington has desert, rainforest, coastline, mountains, rivers, volcanoes, glaciers, and hot springs. Outdoor enthusiasts have flocked to the state to take advantage of the wide range of terrain and the activities that come along with it, including hiking, snow sports, fishing, boating, biking, climbing, and exploring. Whatever adventure you're looking for—from backpacking trips to a beginner's hike—Washington's got it.

OUTDOOR ADVENTURES

1 Ape Cave

GPS Coordinates: N46° 06.519' W122° 12.623'; Mount St. Helens National Volcanic Monument, 42218 NE Yale Bridge Road, Amboy, WA 98601; 360-449-7800
fs.usda.gov/recarea/giffordpinchot/recarea/?recid=40393

Prepare for your underground adventure by wearing a jacket and sturdy shoes (it can be muddy in places, and the cave is 42°F year-round). Bring at least one headlamp or flashlight per person to see where you're walking, and to admire the cave around you. From the parking lot, walk to the cave entrance: a staircase into the ground. If you're up for a challenge, take the upper cave, where you'll scramble over lava rock piles and scale a lava wall (this section is only 1.5 miles but takes about 2.5 hours to hike). You'll know quickly if it's too much for you. If so, head back to the fork at the staircase and set off for the lower cave for a 1.5-mile round-trip walk (many children, especially practiced hikers, are able to do this trail at a slow and careful pace). You'll need a Northwest Forest Pass or $5 day pass April 1–November 30 (and a Sno-Park permit December 1–March 31). Look out for lava stalactites, stalagmites, and other formations.

2 Beacon Rock State Park

34841 WA 14, Skamania, WA 98648; 509-427-8265
parks.state.wa.us/474/beacon-rock

Beacon Rock, which looks like a small but prominent mountain, sits at the edge of the Columbia River. A steep, mile-long switchback trail takes you up and up to the 848-foot summit, providing beautiful vistas along the way. The state park includes a picnic area with a view of Beacon Rock, as well as a campground. The site as a whole is also part of the Lewis and Clark National Historic Trail. The area is known for its hiking, waterfalls, rock climbing, boating, mountain biking, and horseback riding. In other words, adventure awaits.

3 Big Four Ice Caves

Mt. Baker–Snoqualmie National Forest, Darrington Ranger District, 1405 Emens Ave. N., Darrington, WA 98241; 360-436-1155
fs.usda.gov/recarea/mbs/recarea/?recid=17728

The result of avalanches and the mountain's great shadow, Big Four Ice Caves is the United States' lowest-elevation glacier outside of Alaska. It's part of the Cascade Range near Granite Falls, Washington. The trail is a relatively flat 2.2 miles and includes a boardwalk through a marshy area as well as a great view of the caves. Admire the caves from the trail; do not go near, inside, or on top of them, as avalanches and collapses are threats year-round. The blue ice at the caves' opening is a marvel. If it's quiet enough, you can often hear water dripping from within the depths of the ice.

4 Dry Falls

34875 Park Lake Road NE, Coulee City, WA 99115; 509-632-5214
parks.state.wa.us/251/dry-falls

According to my father-in-law, "There's no other place on our planet that displays the forms of erosion in such unimaginable dimensions as are viewed at Dry Falls." You do have to use your imagination, though. This is the site of the world's largest waterfall—3.5 miles wide, with a 400-foot drop—only it's been dried up for thousands of years. Stop in at Dry Falls Visitor Center within the state park to learn about the Missoula Floods, when water cut through Eastern Washington to form the Channeled Scablands and the Grand Coulee, and put regions of multiple states hundreds of feet underwater. Dry Falls Lake and Deep Lake are worthwhile stops to admire the waters or take a dip. If you're up for a drive, take WA 28 south toward Wenatchee. You'll see the Columbia River and the Moses Coulee on the way to Rock Island. I would be surprised if you didn't decide to hike the Moses Coulee Preserve— or at least pull over to admire these beautiful basalt formations.

5 Ephrata Fan

Hatchery Road NE, Soap Lake, WA 98851

It is the incredibly beautiful strata and erratic boulders that awe in eastern Washington; the coulees and scablands look almost otherworldly to me. The Ephrata Fan is a perfect trip for exploration and geology. (See also Dry Falls, above, and Palouse Falls, page 17). Out-of-place-looking boulders the size of armchairs and small cars dot the fields, dropped here during the Missoula Floods. From Moses Lake, head north on WA 17. Turn right onto Hatchery Road and go as if to Troutlodge hatchery. Before you get there, a very large basalt boulder will be on the left side of the road. This area doesn't have developed hiking trails, but hop out to enjoy the boulder fields of thousands of granite and basalt rocks.

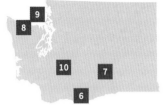

6 Goldendale Observatory State Park

1602 Observatory Drive, Goldendale, WA 98620; 509-773-3141
goldendaleobservatory.com

Stargazers and astronomers, this trip's for you. Bring your camera
and binoculars and take a trip to Goldendale to see the sky like you
haven't before. Goldendale State Park's website explains that they
provide access to one of the largest public telescopes in the country.
The most exciting thing they provide may be the interpretive programs, including afternoon and evening observations on weekends
year-round (included with your Discover Pass). Observe whatever's in
the sky, or plan your visit based on the moon cycle, the Perseid
meteor shower, or another special event. For example, when Mercury
made a rare trip between Earth and the sun in November 2019, the
observatory was open to host the event.

7 Hanford Reach National Monument

Mattawa, WA 99349; 509-546-8300
fws.gov/refuge/hanford_reach

Hanford Reach is the U.S. Fish & Wildlife Service's first national
monument, established in 2000. The site has minimal facilities, and
the area is remote and full of wildlife—wildflowers, mule deer, elk,
and bald eagles, to name a few. The rolling hills, dunes, and bluffs
work together with the Columbia River and Saddle Mountain Lake to
create a quiet refuge. But it's a complicated place. Partly because of
its remote locale, Hanford Reach was chosen as the site to build
the B Reactor, which was used to manufacture plutonium as part of
the Manhattan Project during World War II. Here is where the technology was developed to create the atomic bomb the United States
dropped on Nagasaki, Japan. The Fish & Wildlife Service's website
explains that priorities have shifted to clean the surrounding land
and waters; the long-retired nuclear reactors are now being disas-
sembled. Our history remains. While you can explore on your own
(hiking, kayaking the river, driving around and observing wildlife),
you may want to take a private tour to learn even more (see Hanford
Nuclear Reservation (and B Reactor Tour), page 101).

8 Lake Crescent

416 Lake Crescent Road, Port Angeles, WA 98363; 360-565-3130
nps.gov/olym/planyourvisit/lake-crescent-area-brochure.htm

Known for its clear, brilliant blue and green waters, Lake Crescent is a special spot to visit. Carved from glaciers during the Ice Age, the lake is captivating due to its color and clarity, and the surrounding mountains and trees frame it beautifully. The National Park Service brochure indicates depths of 624 feet. At 11–12 miles long, the lake provides lots of shore to explore (plan to take a least a couple of hours to drive around it, more if you're stopping to hike or swim). You can lounge at the lodge, hike to Marymere Falls, or go swimming at Devil's Punch Bowl along the Spruce Railroad Trail. If you continue on to hike the Fairholme Campground Loop, you might be tempted to turn your day trip into an overnighter. It's certainly not the worst place to wake up.

9 Lime Kiln Point State Park

1567 Westside Road, Friday Harbor, WA 98250; 360-378-2044
parks.state.wa.us/540/lime-kiln-point

From May to September, orca whales are regularly spotted in Haro Strait by San Juan Island. On many lucky days, you can see them from the shore at Lime Kiln Point State Park. If you really want to see some, take a whale-watching tour. The naturalists at San Juan Safaris are knowledgeable, friendly, and respectful of the wildlife. On every trip, 90% of which include whale sightings, you'll learn a lot about the Salish Sea's resident and transient orcas and the research and conservation that has been at work in this area since the 1970s.

10 Paradise, Mount Rainier National Park

52807 Paradise Road E., Ashford, WA 98304; 360-569-2211
nps.gov/mora/planyourvisit/paradise.htm

Visit Mount Rainier National Park and head to Paradise. The wildflowers begin blooming in the spring as the snow melts, and new blossoms steadily appear throughout the summer, changing from lower elevations to alpine heights. Blooming reports are posted at the National Park Service website, but typically mid-July is peak season. Set out for Alta Vista or Skyline Trail. To design your own hike, grab a map from the visitor center—be careful to stay on trails so as not to damage the delicate alpine meadows. You're bound to see avalanche lilies, glacier lilies, Calypso orchids, lily of the valley, lupine, Indian paintbrush, and many more species. Listen for the chirps of marmots and pikas in the rocks as you pass.

Missed this year's flowers? Paradise is the main winter-use area of Mount Rainier National Park. Venture here for cross-country skiing, tubing, and snowshoeing.

11 Sherlock Peak

GPS Coordinates: N48° 52.188' W117° 30.222' (near Colville, WA 99114); 509-684-7000
tinyurl.com/sherlockpeak

You may not encounter another party on the trail during this 7-mile round-trip hike. The Selkirk Range in northeast Washington State feels incredibly remote. Stretching into northern Idaho and British Columbia, Canada, it is home to many animals, including birds of prey, cougars, grizzlies, mule deer, bighorn sheep, and gray wolves. If you go in late summer/early fall, huckleberries will be plentiful along the trail. You may catch wildflowers in August. The trail has been described as rugged, but it is well marked and provides beautiful 360-degree views of the range at the summit (6,200 feet elevation, as documented by the Washington Trails Association). Other mountains in the range reach heights upward of 10,000 feet. This goes without saying, but be sure to pack enough water and snacks. Always snacks.

12 Snow Lake

GPS Coordinates: N47° 27.851' W121° 26.804' (near North Bend, WA 98045); 425-888-1421
tinyurl.com/snowlakehike

Snow Lake has views that wow whether it's sunny or foggy. It's no wonder that so many people hit this trail again and again. The alpine lake, the snowcapped mountains dotted with conifers—it's a glorious sight. That said, if you can go on a nonsummer weekday, the trail (and parking lot) will feel a little freer. At 7.2 miles round-trip with an 1,800-foot elevation gain, the hike is not nearly as tough as some others in the region, but it's not nothing either. If you get a sunny day, there is almost no shade on the trail, so don't forget a hat and sunscreen. Plan to spend 3–4 hours hiking, depending on your pace, and an hour taking in the views.

A springtime view of Twin Sisters Rock, complete with foreground flora

13 **Twin Sisters Rock**

GPS Coordinates: N46° 02.556' W118° 56.424' (US 730, Kennewick, WA 99337)

Twin Sisters Rock can be spotted from the road as you're driving by. In fact, there's no missing it. It's the kind of formation that makes you wonder, "What is that and what is it doing here?" The Sisters are two basalt columns sitting side by side, part of the Columbia River Basalt Group, which, according to the U.S. Geological Survey, was part of the most recent, and most well-preserved, massive fissure basalt flows. The Missoula Floods contributed to the erosion, separating the basalt into two. You can hike 0.5 mile up the main trail to the base of Twin Sisters and admire them from a close vantage (climbing the rocks is not permitted). From the top of the hill, take in the panoramic view of the Columbia River and Wallula Gap.

Snoqualmie Falls (see page 19)

WHO DOESN'T LOVE A WATERFALL? Washington State has
no shortage; the count falls somewhere in the thousands. Many
are located on the western side of the state, but Palouse Falls
in eastern Washington is well worth the drive, no matter where
you're coming from. Whatever you're looking for—height, volume
of water, the surrounding beauty, a long hike to a secluded spot,
a dog-friendly area, or an ADA-friendly view—there is something
for you here.

WATERFALLS

1 Bridal Veil Falls

GPS Coordinates: N47° 48.552' W121° 34.440' (US 2, Gold Bar, WA 98251); 360-677-2414
tinyurl.com/mbsnationalforest; wta.org/go-hiking/hikes/bridal-veil-falls

The hike to the falls, with 1,000 feet of elevation gain and a bit of a scramble, may not be suited for everyone. From the base of the falls at the end of the trail, enjoy the spray of water in the air and the view up the sheer rock face—this waterfall flows year-round. Washington Trails Association reports that Bridal Veil Falls takes a 100-foot drop down the east wall of Mount Index. This is just one of seven drops the waterfall plummets, totaling 1,291 feet according to the Northwest Waterfall Survey. Unfortunately, you won't see all seven tiers at once. Should you find yourself in need of a longer hike, trek the mile back down to the main trail where it forks up to Lake Serene, which feeds the falls. It's an even longer, steeper climb but worth it for the vista at the lake.

2 Falls Creek Falls

GPS Coordinates: N45° 54.561' W121° 54.762' (Forest Service Road 57, Carson, WA 98610); 509-395-3400
tinyurl.com/fallscreektrail; www.waterfallsnorthwest.com/waterfall/falls-creek-falls-5245

Falls upon falls upon falls! Falls Creek Falls is a multitiered waterfall stretching up 335 feet, according to the Northwest Waterfall Survey. Take in all three tiers after hiking the wide path up a steady incline to the falls. You can opt to hike the upper loop as well. The upper loop trail may be slightly less well maintained, but it provides beautiful greenery and more viewpoints from which to enjoy the falls. These falls flow year-round, and the trail is suitable for children with some hiking experience.

3 Franklin Falls

GPS Coordinates (for trailhead): N47° 24.786' W121° 26.553' (Forest Service Road 5830, North Bend, WA 98045); 425-888-1421
tinyurl.com/franklinfallstrail; wta.org/go-hiking/hikes/franklin-falls

Franklin Falls is a short hike, at only 2 miles round-trip. The elevation gain is minimal (400 feet), making this a great hike for children, folks new to hiking, or those looking for something relatively easy. The Washington Trails Association reports the heaviest water flow from April to July, making for an impressive plunge pool and spray. Water continues to flow through the winter season, when icicle formations create an additional layer of beauty.

4 Myrtle Falls, Mount Rainier

52807 Paradise Road E., Ashford, WA 98304; 360-569-2211
nps.gov/mora/planyourvisit/paradise.htm; visitrainier.com/myrtle-falls

Fed by the Nisqually River, this sizable horsetail waterfall fans out along the rock face as it cascades down to Edith Creek. Myrtle Falls is eye-catching with or without the views of Mount Rainier behind it (but cross your fingers for a clear day because wow!). If you leave from the Paradise Visitors Center at Mount Rainier, this is an easy 0.8-mile round-trip hike on a paved trail. The payoff is one of the most iconic views of Mount Rainier National Park. According to the National Park Service, the Skyline Trail to Myrtle Falls is accessible to wheelchairs with assistance. Note that there is a 100-foot elevation gain.

5 Palouse Falls

GPS Coordinates: N46° 39.837' W118° 17.844' (Palouse Falls Road, LaCrosse, WA 99143); 509-646-9218
parks.state.wa.us/559/palouse-falls

In 2014 Palouse Falls was designated Washington's official state waterfall. This is a plunge waterfall that drops from nearly 200 feet into a pool below. When the sun is at the right angle, a rainbow emerges in the mist. You can see the falls and their spray from the parking lot across the canyon, falling amid basalt cliffs. The canyon itself was carved during the Missoula Floods. While tempting, the hike down to the pool at the base of the falls is extremely dangerous. Adventurers are encouraged to enjoy the falls and their surroundings from the vantage above.

Palouse Falls is also Washington's state waterfall (see page 152).

6 Panther Creek Falls

GPS Coordinates (for trailhead): N45° 52.045' W121° 49.587' (Forest Service Road 65, Carson, WA 98610); 509-395-3400
tinyurl.com/pantherfallshike

Climb 100 feet up a very short trail (0.16 mile round-trip) to the viewing deck at Panther Creek Falls, a collection of tiered horsetail waterfalls about 100 feet wide and 136 feet tall, according to the Northwest Waterfall Survey. Because these falls spill over such a wide swath of rock, they are particularly mesmerizing to stare into. Vibrant greens from the moss and trees give the impression of a fairy's paradise. Once you've enjoyed the view from the observation deck, check out the trail that leads down toward the base of the waterfall. Improvements were made to provide a safer experience.

7 Rainbow Falls

GPS Coordinates: N48° 20.532' W120° 42.078' (Stehekin Valley Road, Stehekin, WA 98852); 360-854-7200
nps.gov/noca/planyourvisit/rainbow-loop-trail.htm; wta.org/go-hiking/hikes/rainbow-falls-mist-trail

Part of both North Cascades National Park and Lake Chelan National Recreation Area, Rainbow Falls is a tucked-away gem. If you haven't yet been to Stehekin, you need to get there. The town itself is remote with a year-round population of 100 people, give or take. You cannot drive there; you need to fly, hike, or boat in. Likely, you'll want to take the fast ferry (2.5 hours each way)—especially if you're only going for the day. Once you're in Stehekin, the Rainbow Falls Mist Trail lets you view the 312-foot-tall waterfall with only 0.25 mile of hiking involved. There's also the Rainbow Loop Trail, which gives you the opportunity for a longer hike (4.4 miles). Any of the trailheads are accessible by bus, shuttle, or bicycle. You can.swim in the pool at the base of the falls if you are so compelled.

8 Skookum Falls

GPS Coordinates: N47° 03.173' W121° 34.417' (WA 410, Enumclaw, WA 98022) (GPS Trailhead Coordinates: N47° 01.334' W121° 32.132'); 360-825-6585
tinyurl.com/skookumfallshike

Technically, Skookum Falls is visible from a marked viewpoint on Chinook Pass (WA 410), but the steep scramble up to see it from the hiking trail makes for much more fun (if you're up for it). The hike to the split to the falls is fairly flat—a lovely meandering forest walk on a soft trail. You can start at the Skookum Flats North Trailhead on Forest Service Road 73, which will give you a 4.2-mile round-trip hike if you hike back out after viewing the falls. Alternately, use the trailhead on FS 7160 for a longer hike, nearly 8 miles round-trip. From either direction, when you hear the sound of rushing water, look for the FALLS sign pointing up. Begin the steep climb, and mind the scree and roots. You'll probably stop for a break or two and wonder if it's worth it to keep going. While I pondered this question, another hiker passed us and then came right back with a report: Keep going. It's worth it. The falls are heaviest in the spring, but even then it's not the water that wows, but the double horsetail drops. According to the Northwest Waterfall Survey, the two visible drops of the falls total 366 feet. Oh, and be careful scooting back down.

9 Snoqualmie Falls

Upper Parking Lot: 6501 Railroad Ave. SE, Snoqualmie, WA 98024
Lower Parking Lot: 37479 SE Fish Hatchery Road, Fall City, WA 98024
snoqualmiefalls.com

Visited by over 1.5 million people each year, Snoqualmie Falls is a *big* attraction. In addition to being the home of Salish Lodge and Snoqualmie Falls Candy Shoppe, the falls have been a source of clean, renewable energy since 1898, when the world's first underground power plant was built, according to Puget Sound Energy. You can learn more at the Hydroelectric Museum, less than a mile down the road from the free upper parking lot at Snoqualmie Falls. There are upper and lower viewing areas for the falls, with a trail in between. The lower trail may be a bit steep for some, but it's a short walk (about 0.7 mile). The water plunges 268 feet into the Snoqualmie River below. While the volume of the falls can vary, during early winter and spring the water spans 100 feet. As you gaze at the falls, you might realize you recognize them from the closing credits of *Twin Peaks*. (Pro tip, *Twin Peaks* lovers: Drive another 5 miles down the road to Twede's Cafe for a piece of pie—and a damn fine cup of coffee.)

10 Sol Duc Falls

GPS Coordinates: N47° 57.315′ W123° 50.151′ (Sol Duc Road, Port Angeles, WA 98362); 360-565-3131
nps.gov/olym/planyourvisit/visiting-the-sol-duc-valley.htm;
wta.org/go-hiking/hikes/sol-duc-falls

The less-than-a-mile-long trail to Sol Duc Falls snakes through old-growth forest. As is the case in most of Olympic National Park, there are mosses, lichens, and liverworts aplenty. The rainforest is always lush and green, a most welcome sight if you're escaping a city. You'll hear the falls before you see them. When they come into view, there could be up to four streams of water gushing into the lower canyon. Maybe more exciting than the falls are the Sol Duc Hot Springs, a couple of miles from the trailhead. If you have time for a soak, enjoy the facilities of the pool and tubs (open late March–late October; dates shift slightly each year). The name Sol Duc comes from the Quileute name, meaning "sparkling water." The Sol Duc River is also a popular destination for rafting and kayaking.

11 Wallace Falls

14503 Wallace Lake Road, Gold Bar, WA 98251; 360-793-0420
parks.state.wa.us/289/wallace-falls

The old-growth forest at Wallace Falls is breathtaking. This may be my favorite state park. To get to the waterfall, head right when the trail splits, and walk along the river to Lower Falls, Middle Falls, and Upper Falls (there are viewpoints at each). The falls drop 265 feet, gather in a pool, and drop again, bringing the total plunge to 367 feet, as documented by the Northwest Waterfall Survey. There are nine waterfalls in all, so if you've had your fill and hiked long enough, head back at any time. Even stopping at Lower Falls is a worthwhile day trip! If you decide to continue up the switchbacks, you'll gain about 1,300 feet of elevation. The trail is 5.6 miles round-trip, or 9 miles if you do the loop up to Wallace Lake and back around. (If you're planning to hike the Wallace Falls Lake Loop, visit wta.org/go-hiking/hikes/wallace-falls-lake-loop for detailed directions.) The full loop offers even more stunning forest and some views, if it's clear. If it's rainy or overcast, this hike is still absolutely beautiful.

The area surrounding Sol Duc Falls in Olympic National Park teems with lush, green plant life.

Mukilteo Lighthouse (see page 25) is unique in its Victorian style and wood construction.

AS SOON AS LARGE SHIPS BEGAN sailing to Washington, large ships began wrecking in Washington. Installing lighthouses throughout the region became increasingly important to guide ships to shore around dangerous capes and sandbars. Cape Disappointment Light was first lit in 1856. Lighthouses were installed and lit on the peninsula and throughout Puget Sound over the next several decades. Some have been destroyed or demolished, but many are still active today—some even doubling as museums.

LIGHTHOUSES

1 Admiralty Head Lighthouse

1280 Engle Road, Coupeville, WA 98239; 360-678-1186
parks.state.wa.us/505/fort-casey

Fort Casey, one of the forts tasked with protecting Puget Sound during World War I and World War II, is the home of Admiralty Head Lighthouse on Whidbey Island. The lighthouse sits at the eastern edge of Admiralty Inlet, off the Strait of Juan de Fuca. It's a brick-and-stucco structure that has changed quite a bit since its early days in 1861, when it first turned its light on (as Red Bluff Lighthouse). While the lighthouse is no longer operational, it is open seasonally and contains a gift shop. In addition to reading signage in the exhibit and admiring the Fresnel lens and lantern room, you can schedule a tour (at the number above) to learn more. Admiralty Head Lighthouse, like many in the region, has a rich history of keepers, owners, and restoration—done in part, in this case, by students from a trio of high school metal-shop classes.

2 Alki Point Lighthouse

3200 Point Place SW, Seattle, WA 98116; 206-841-3519
tinyurl.com/alkiptlighthouse

Painted white with green trim and red roofs, Alki Point Lighthouse still guides maritime traffic into Elliott Bay. The lighthouse is located on Alki Beach in West Seattle, on Duwamish lands. There is free admission and tours throughout the summer thanks to the U.S. Coast Guard auxiliarists who lead them. It was on one of these tours that I first learned of the science behind the mighty Fresnel lens. The Fresnel lens is an incredible piece of engineering in which many ridged lenses are situated to capture light and focus it into a single, powerful beam that shines out in one direction. Before there was a lighthouse with a light that could be seen 12 miles away, there was—the story goes—a kerosene lantern that Hans Martin Hanson hung on the side of his barn as a courtesy in the 1870s. It was upgraded slightly in 1887 thanks to the U.S. Lighthouse Service, but it was still just a lantern on a post. It wasn't until 1913 that the lighthouse and its keepers' houses were built and ready to operate. If you plan your trip so that you can take a tour, you have the privilege of climbing the tight spiral staircase up to the tower to take in the view of Puget Sound. Imagine being tasked to operate the lens, hand-cranking its turning mechanism every so often, for a 12-hour shift.

3 Cape Disappointment Lighthouse

244 Robert Gray Drive, Ilwaco, WA 98624; 360-642-3078
parks.state.wa.us/486/cape-disappointment

Marking the entrance to the Columbia River, Cape Disappointment Lighthouse first went into operation in 1856, after some years of construction setbacks, including a ship full of building materials wrecking as it tried to cross the river bar. It's no wonder this stretch of coast earned the nickname Graveyard of the Pacific. So many ships wrecked here that one of the keepers, J. W. Munson, took it upon himself to fix up and maintain a lifesaving boat. His work eventually led to a lifesaving station, established in 1871. This tradition continues today through the U.S. Coast Guard Station at Cape Disappointment.

Cape Disappointment Lighthouse eventually got a black band around its tower to distinguish it from North Head Lighthouse. North Head was completed in 1898 to guide ships traveling from the north that had an obstructed view of Cape Disappointment. You can see these lighthouses—both still active navigational aids—at Cape Disappointment State Park, where there is also a Lewis & Clark Interpretive Center.

4 Mukilteo Lighthouse

608 Front St., Mukilteo, WA 98275; 425-263-8180
mukilteowa.gov/departments/recreation/parks-open-spaces-trails/lighthouse-park

Located on Point Elliott, Mukilteo Lighthouse is part of Lighthouse Park, which is owned and operated by the City of Mukilteo. The lighthouse has been aiding navigation since 1906. It has a Victorian design and is made of wood—most others on the Puget Sound are constructed from brick, stucco, and concrete. The interior and grounds are open to the public, and admission is free.

The Treaty of Point Elliott was signed in Mukilteo in 1855, very near the site of Lighthouse Park, where the Mukilteo Lighthouse stands today. Broadly, the treaty protects Indigenous Americans' hunting and fishing rights and establishes reservations in exchange for land for European American settlers. Because the European American settlers failed to fulfill their treaty obligations, rebellions began later that year and lasted through 1858. The treaty was ratified in 1859, but to this day European Americans have not fulfilled the obligations of the Treaty of Point Elliott. The full text of the treaty is available online (goia.wa.gov/tribal-government/treaty-point-elliott-1855).

Lighthouses

5 New Dungeness Lighthouse

554 Voice of America Road W., Sequim, WA 98382; 360-683-6638
newdungenesslighthouse.com

New Dungeness Lighthouse sits at the end of a 5-mile-long spit in Dungeness National Wildlife Refuge. First lit in 1857 to guide ships through the Strait of Juan de Fuca, it is still in operation today. Hiking the spit at high tide is not advisable; check the tide table before you set out. You must hike in the open elements, so dress accordingly and wear sunscreen. If you decide to turn your day trip into a week-long adventure, there is a unique opportunity to be a lighthouse keeper (accompanying children must be age 6 or older). You won't have to stay awake overnight as the lighthouse is automated now, but you will give tours and perform other duties. It's thanks to volunteers that the lighthouse is still open today. If you make the hike to the end of the spit, it's a volunteer who will greet you and give you a tour.

A sunny day at Cape Disappointment Lighthouse, Ilwaco

Siouxon Creek Falls (see page 38)

A COASTAL STATE WITH MANY WATERWAYS, Washington boasts beaches and swimming holes galore. There is the wild beach of the coast on the far western edge of the United States, the beaches along Puget Sound and its islands, and a plethora of lakes and rivers. Tide pools are home to anemones, sea stars, barnacles, and crabs. Sand dollar and sea glass hunters can walk the sands in search of treasures. Thrill seekers can cliff jump into a clear pool of glacial water. You can also clam, swim, paddleboard, kayak, boogie board, skim board, surf, or get in a game of volleyball.

BEACHES AND SWIMMING HOLES

(continued on next page)

29

Sea stacks at Ruby Beach (see page 14), located on the Olympic Peninsula, part of Olympic National Park

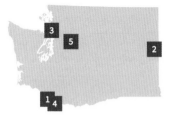

1 Battle Ground Lake State Park

18002 NE 249th St., Battle Ground, WA 98604; 360-687-4621
parks.state.wa.us/472/battle-ground-lake

This 280-acre state park includes a campground and opportunities
for hiking, biking, (nonmotorized) boating, fishing, and scuba diving.
But we're here to swim. The spring-fed lake has a very shallow area
for tentative swimmers (read: great for children). The beach area is
pretty, with some sand at the shoreline and a grassy area for lounging and picnicking. The water is a beautiful turquoise-green color,
especially in the right light. The park has just renovated to provide
more-accessible entrances at the boat launch and dock, as well as
an ADA-friendly fishing pier. This is a lovely spot for a dip!

2 Boulder Beach Park

GPS Coordinates: N47° 41.683' W117° 18.486' (East Upriver Drive, Spokane,
WA 99217); 509-535-7084
www.spokaneriver.net/watertrail/park-details/?parkID=203

You might not know about Boulder Beach if you're new to the area.
But once you find it, it will likely be a go-to spot for a summer swim
day. And if you grew up here, you already know that Boulder Beach
sits on the north bank of the Spokane River on Upriver Drive. It's
pretty chill as far as close-to-city swimming holes go. I went here
after a round of disc golf at the course nearby in Camp Sekani Park.
The river is calm—almost lakelike—at this stretch. People fish
from the boulders, and kayakers use this as a put-in spot. If you're
traveling by bicycle, you can access the beach from the Centennial
Trail. Cool off!

3 Cama Beach Historical State Park

1880 W. Camano Drive, Camano Island, WA 98282; 360-387-1550
parks.state.wa.us/483/cama-beach

A dreamy island beach without taking a ferry ride? Yes, please! The
WA 532 bridge connects Camano Island to the mainland (and to I-5).
The island reaches south into Puget Sound from there. Cama Beach
Historical State Park is about 20 minutes from the bridge, with

Camano Island State Park just a little farther south (you can walk the mile-long trail to the other park). The Center for Wooden Boats at the state park has free admission and is worth checking out (highly recommend!). It also has boat rentals available.

If you're just here to swim, then get to it! There are some large pieces of driftwood to sit on or lean against if you're waiting to work up the nerve to jump in the water. The beach is a little rocky in some areas (small rocks, not boulders, but don't expect smooth, fine sand). The water is cold, yes, but very, very refreshing.

4 Dougan Falls

GPS Coordinates: N45° 40.362' W122° 09.189' (Washougal River Road, Washougal, WA 98671)
www.waterfallsnorthwest.com/waterfall/dougan-creek-falls-3122

Talk about a swimming hole! This is a glorious pool of water at the base of Dougan Creek Falls. The waterfall is only 12 feet high but about twice as wide. It is a gentle cascade into the lovely blue-green water below. There's a camping area nearby, but coming just for the swim would be my pick for this spot. The water is really clear—you can see about 20 feet down by my estimate. If it's too crowded, another day-use swimming area is nearby, but you're really going to want to be at the falls.

5 Eagle Falls

GPS Coordinates: N47° 47.749' W121° 30.826' (US 2, Gold Bar, WA 98251); 360-677-2414
fs.usda.gov/mbs; outdoorproject.com/united-states/washington /eagle-falls-swimming-hole

Snohomish County does not disappoint. I love swimming through a gorge, and Eagle Falls is a great spot for it. The rock formations along the river are impressive—very cool shapes and curves. Located not far off of US 2, on the South Fork Skykomish River, Eagle Falls drops into the basin below. The waters are glacial, so get ready for a shock to your system. The 20-foot-deep pools and rocky outcrops are tempting spots for cliff jumping, but do so only with extreme caution. The wow factors here are the rocks and the glacial-turquoise water.

If you want an extra stop, check out Big Eddy Park and its sandy beach, about 8.5 miles west of Eagle Falls.

6 Elwha River

Olympic Hot Springs Road and Whiskey Bend Road, Port Angeles, WA 98363;
360-565-3130
nps.gov/olym/learn/nature/elwha-ecosystem-restoration.htm

How is Washington State so pretty? I actually ask myself this on a regular basis. But the Elwha River is one reason. With a complicated history of dams installed and removed (see Glines Canyon Dam Removal Site, page 83), the river is free now, trying to return to a natural state. It's one of those special places in the state where the water is blue green and unreal. There are certainly lots of spots where you can swim along the river, but this one is ideal. The water slows to create a large basin of cool, clear water along Olympic Hot Springs Road, about 1.25 miles south of the Elwha Ranger Station (look for the narrow dirt road that forks to the left). The water levels vary, but cliff jumping is a favorite pastime here (when you can see that it's safe). Even if everyone else goes swimming and you merely dip your toes in the chilly, chilly water, I'd still consider that a swimming success. Because look how pretty it is!

7 Fort Worden State Park

200 Battery Way, Port Townsend, WA 98368; 360-344-4400
fortworden.org

I have been to Fort Worden State Park at least seven times and—somehow—have gone swimming only once! To be fair, sometimes it was not the season for swimming, but other times I just enjoyed walks on the beach. Once an active Army base, the state park itself is huge—434 acres. There are old structures to explore, officers' houses to admire (or rent), and an active lighthouse facing the Strait of Juan de Fuca. You can explore by hiking the trails and overlooking the sound from the bluff, or head straight to the beach.

The beach has fine sand and some driftwood logs back toward the grassy area. There is lots of exploring to be done at low tide (you can walk all the way downtown). If you'd prefer to be on the water rather than in it, you can rent a kayak, and there is a dock if you are look-ing to go fishing or crabbing. Or just lounge and swim. Read a book, get toasty, jump in the water, reapply sunscreen; read a book, get toasty, jump in the water, reapply sunscreen. That is what I would do if I weren't walking past the tableau of dead crabs. Well done, seagulls. Well done.

8 | Long Beach

Long Beach, WA 98631; 360-642-2400
visitlongbeachpeninsula.com

What a beach! The first time I went to Long Beach, it was November. When I first arrived, I went straight to the water, even though it was approaching midnight. It's one of those beaches that feels so open and wild—certainly the storm brewing contributed to the dramatic effect I was experiencing. That said, this beach isn't for weak swimmers. In fact, swimming in general is not recommended, and especially not for children. There are no lifeguards, and sneaker waves are common, even on seemingly calm days. So why am I including Long Beach as a day trip? Because it is still worth it to go here! The beach is beautiful. Play on the sand and enjoy the sound of the water. If you must swim, wear your wetsuit—the waters are all kinds of cold (ranging from 45°F to 60°F)—and your personal flotation device (PFD). This is also an excellent surfing beach (in a wetsuit). There are surf lessons in the area for beginner and intermediate surfers. Long Beach is a beach that many would prefer to enjoy in a dry capacity—and I don't blame them.

9 | Ocean Shores

Ocean Shores, WA 98569; 360-289-9586
tourismoceanshores.com

With 6 miles of wide-open sandy beach, Ocean Shores is a little coastal dream. If you read the previous entry (Long Beach), this one is a bit similar in that swimming isn't necessarily the number one thing to do here, and it isn't recommended. The rip currents can be rather fierce, and the water is cold. However, you can charter a boat to fish for tuna, fly a kite, built a sandcastle, go clamming, or rent an electric fat-tire bike to ride on the packed sand. Bring your beach games and your umbrellas and have a fun day listening to the waves roar and crash. If you're without wee ones, a trip to North Jetty Beach at Ocean Shores is worthwhile for the view. The coastline is wild, rocky, and stunning.

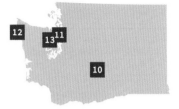

Beaches and
Swimming Holes

10 Pacman Cliff

GPS Coordinates: N46° 49.718' W120° 27.665' (WA 821, Ellensburg, WA 98926)
redsflyshop.com/how-to-float-yakima-river

Formerly known as Smiley Face, Pacman Cliff is a spot along the
Yakima River. I typically take to the river in an inner tube at Umtanum Creek, but you can get to Pacman however you want. From
Umtanum Creek Recreation Area, drive south on Canyon Road about
3 miles; there is a large graffitied Pacman on the rocks to mark the
spot. The water here is relatively calm (Class 1), and there's a nice
wide area for boats and rafts to pass, and for you to swim.

There are a couple of spots where daredevils could cliff jump, a lower
cliff and an upper one. Be sure the water levels are deep enough
(at least 13 feet), and wear water shoes or sneakers. Always cliff
jump responsibly. Alternately, climb down and go for a swim!

11 Point No Point

9009 Point No Point Road NE, Hansville, WA 98340; 415-362-7255
kitsapgov.com/parks/Pages/PointNoPointPark.aspx

Point No Point is the northernmost point—yeah, I said it—of Kitsap
Peninsula. Check out Puget Sound's oldest lighthouse, Point No
Point Lighthouse (open to visitors on weekends), and build your
own driftwood structure (or enhance someone else's). This sandy
beach beckons blankets to be laid out, kites to be flown, and sand-
castles to be built. I hear it's a good salmon fishing spot too. Walk
along the beach, choose a lounging spot, or hike to the wetland trail
behind the lighthouse keeper's quarters to spot some birds or other
wildlife. However you decide to spend the day here, it's bound to be
a good one.

12 Rialto Beach

GPS Coordinates: N47° 55.285' W124° 38.285' (western terminus of Mora Road, Forks, WA 98331); 360-565-3130
nps.gov/olym/planyourvisit/rialto-beach.htm

This spot makes me swoon. It's something about the unadulterated wilderness. Picture undeveloped coastline with a beach that moves from small round stones to sand. Picture the tall windblown trees looking out at the water, and their equally gigantic fallen counterparts, now sun-bleached driftwood. Walk south for a view of the islands, and north to Hole-in-the-Wall. (*Note:* Leashed dogs are allowed only as far north as Ellen Creek.) If you catch low tide, anemones, sea stars, crabs, and little fish are easy to search for and observe in the tide pools. The sea stacks make for amazing photographs. The beach continues undeveloped for some 30 miles, but you can either turn back here; find a spot to sit; (carefully) wade in the surf; or cross your fingers that you might see otters, whales, sea lions, seals, or eagles.

If you're already in the area, get all your *Twilight* visits out of the way at La Push and Forks. And consider checking out Ruby Beach, First Beach, Second Beach, and Third Beach. All the beaches! While the wild coast isn't an ideal place for a swim, it's a great spot to admire the ocean.

13 Rocky Brook Falls

2405 Dosewallips Road, Brinnon, WA 98320; 360-452-8552
olympicpeninsulawaterfalltrail.com/rocky-brook-falls
www.waterfallsnorthwest.com/waterfall/rocky-brook-falls-3212

Just a couple hundred yards from the parking pullout, Rocky Brook Falls is a 229-foot-tall horsetail waterfall, according to Northwest Waterfall Survey. In the summer months, the green-blue waters pooling at the base of the falls are particularly inviting. There isn't *too* much space here—so don't expect a large beach—but there's plenty of room for a few parties to enjoy the water. You can wade around or swim a bit, but avoid cliff jumping here. There are a lot of shallow areas and the pool is well-contained, so it should prove a good spot for newer swimmers (always supervise children and bring personal flotation devices for those who aren't strong swimmers).

Beaches and
Swimming Holes

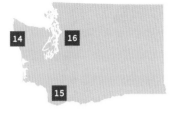

Beaches and Swimming Holes

14 Ruby Beach

GPS Coordinates: N47° 42.448' W124° 24.834' (US 101, Forks, WA 98331);
360-565-3130
nps.gov/olym/planyourvisit/visiting-kalaloch-and-ruby-beach.htm

Is this the prettiest beach in Washington? Maybe. Ruby Beach is a
big, beautiful, remote sandy beach in Olympic National Park, complete with sea stacks, driftwood, and undeveloped coastline. You've
got to be committed to make this a day trip—it's about 2 hours and
45 minutes from Port Townsend, and 2 hours and 20 minutes from
Olympia—but it's worth every minute of the drive. The tide pools
have brightly colored anemones, sea stars, and barnacles. The surf is
beautiful and unruly (not the best spot to swim), but at low tide there
are often little pools you could wade around or sit in. I could sit here
and stare into the ocean for hours. I mean, I'm waiting to see a
whale, but still, the view and the sound of the waves is soul-filling.
The clouds, the sea stacks, the setting sun—it really doesn't get
much better.

And if you've made it this far to the coast, consider stopping by to
admire Rialto Beach (and First, Second, and Third Beaches, page 37)
as well.

15 Siouxon Creek

GPS Coordinates: N45° 56.795' W122° 10.657' (eastern terminus of Forest Service
Road 5701, Amboy, WA 98601); 509-395-3400
tinyurl.com/siouxoncreek; wta.org/go-hiking/hikes/siouxon

Siouxon Creek (pronounced "soo-sahn") is nestled in Gifford Pinchot
National Forest and is absolutely stunning. The waters are emerald
green and so clear you can typically see straight down 15–20 feet.
There are a number of choice swimming holes along the creek, complete with little waterfalls that only add to the majesty. You'll hike
about 5 miles through old-growth forest to get to the first waterfall
with a large swimming hole. Certainly jump in here. In fact, even if
you turn back now, you'll have had a full day and an amazingly
refreshing swim. If you're turning your day trip into an overnight
camping adventure—or are coming from closer to Gifford Pinchot

than I am—you may want to keep hiking to the next few falls. There are more opportunities to swim, of course, and it just gets more and more picturesque. The lush green moss and ferns covering the forest floor and the green water are all very inviting. Usually during summer days, the sun gleams down on the water's surface (hopefully warming it up a bit). Check with the Mount Adams Ranger District for updates on the road conditions.

16 Skykomish River, Big Eddy Park

GPS Coordinates: N47° 50.161' W121° 39.564' (US 2, Gold Bar, WA 98251); 360-793-0420
wdfw.wa.gov/places-to-go/water-access-sites/30537;
parks.state.wa.us/289/wallace-falls

Access the Skykomish River on the right side of the bridge when you're coming from Gold Bar. Big Eddy Park is one of those places that seem to invite you in. The Skykomish River flows here in its bright turquoise tones, but not too quickly, and man-made rock walls section off areas of the water where you can hang out and where less confident swimmers can feel a bit safer. You might relax on the shore at the picnic table or go for a little breaststroke. The Skykomish is fed from the Cascades, so the water is cold, making this a great place to go on a hot summer day. Did I mention this river also has a sandy beach? It's just a really, really nice spot.

Another 8.5 miles east of Big Eddy is Eagle Falls—an area with very cool rock formations and deep pools of clear turquoise water.

Museum of Glass (see page 42)

LOOKING FOR AN EXPERIENTIAL MUSEUM? A specialty
area? We've got pinball machines; we've got glassmaking; we've
got electricity. I like to think these particular museum visits are
fun for solo visitors, families, couples, and pals alike. Relish the
learning that comes through interaction at Spark, or geek out
about Dave Chihuly's magical, tentacle-like glass chandeliers
and try to remember where you've seen one before.

SPECIALTY MUSEUMS

Specialty
Museums

1 Living Computers Museum + Labs

2245 First Ave. S., Seattle, WA 98134; 206-342-2020
livingcomputers.org

Tech geeks and everyday users alike will enjoy a nostalgic dive into every type of computing technology they've ever experienced, much of it interactive, or just get the satisfaction of knowing that their kids understand what a floppy drive is. This museum is a great place to reflect on the past and future of technology.

2 Museum of Glass

1801 Dock St., Tacoma, WA 98402; 253-284-4750
museumofglass.org

This museum covers a breathtaking 75,000 square feet in which you can explore and admire the art of glassmaking.

3 Seattle Children's Museum

305 Harrison St., Seattle, WA 98109; 206-441-1768
thechildrensmuseum.org

Inspiring curiosity in kids age 8 and under, this hands-on museum lets little ones learn and explore the world around them.

4 Seattle Pinball Museum

508 Maynard Ave. S., Seattle, WA 98104; 206-623-0759
seattlepinballmuseum.com

This little museum is all about sharing the love of pinball. It has more than 50 pinball machines—to play!

5 Spark Museum of Electrical Invention

1312 Bay St., Bellingham, WA 98225; 360-738-3886
sparkmuseum.org

Interactive experiential exhibits make Spark a fun stop in Bellingham. In addition to the art, there are special hosted shows and events. Get in there, inventors (and consumers of inventions).

Can you believe for the price of admission you get to play unlimited pinball games

The Tropical Butterfly House at Seattle's Pacific Science Center (see page 47)

WHETHER YOU HAVE LIVED in Washington State for ages, are new to the area, or are only here on a brief visit, these museums provide a good peek into our region. There's a mix of art, history, geology, and culture represented here. I hope you dig in and get a little glimpse into the Northwest. You might be interested in the gold rush or the Missoula Floods, petrified wood or whales. Either way, I do hope you will give these museums a try. They are worth driving across the state for. *See also Indigenous Peoples' Museums, page 95, and Washington State History, page 99.*

REGIONAL MUSEUMS

1 Burke Museum

4300 15th Ave. NE, Seattle, WA 98105; 206-543-7907
burkemuseum.org

Founded by the Young Naturalists in 1885, the Burke Museum reopened in 2019 after undergoing a massive rejuvenation, including a new building and a redesigning of the museum experience. That experience connects visitors to the historical and living natural and cultural diversity of the Pacific Northwest through interactive exhibits. For its external and internal renovation, the museum worked with Indigenous communities to make the visitor experience more respectful and relevant. The new focus on interactivity makes this an especially fun day trip for families with school-age kids. The New Burke is conveniently located in the U District (close to a light-rail station that is scheduled to open in 2021).

2 Coastal Interpretive Center

1033 Catala Ave. SE, Ocean Shores, WA 98569; 360-289-4617
interpretivecenter.org

Stop in for some info about coastal environments on your way to the beaches, snag a selfie with the giant seahorse, try to memorize shells you're sure to find on the beach, and prepare yourself for a lot of up-close taxidermy.

3 Ginkgo Petrified Forest Interpretive Center

4511 Huntzinger Road., Vantage, WA 98950; 509-856-2290
parks.state.wa.us/1113/ginkgo-petrified-forest

Unlike any other museum you can visit, this one takes you on mind-bending paths weaving through giant petrified logs strewn across a desert hillside, some so well preserved that it's hard to believe they're made of stone. Look out over the Columbia River, and see types of petrified wood from all over the world in the visitor center. Bonus points if you can find the saber-toothed tiger skull.

4 Klondike Gold Rush National Historical Park

319 Second Ave. S., Seattle, WA 98104; 206-220-4240
nps.gov/klse

Roam two stories of exhibits as you learn how this gold-based boom helped shape the city and region. Ponder what you would have included in your grubstake, and imagine what your fate might have been, had you been brave enough to join the tide hoping to get rich quick. Did I mention it's free, in the city, and staffed with national park rangers who can answer all your other Washington national park questions? Rush on over!

5 Northwest African American Museum

2300 S. Massachusetts St., Seattle, WA 98144; 206-518-6000
naamnw.org

Enjoy and learn about the history, culture, and art of people of African descent in the Pacific Northwest. Regular exhibitions tell the stories of black people who were brought to the continent through slavery, as well as those of recent immigrants, and showcase the work of black artists.

6 Northwest Museum of Arts and Culture

2316 W. First Ave., Spokane, WA 99201; 509-456-3931
northwestmuseum.org

This Inland Northwest museum includes a mansion tour in addition to permanent and featured exhibits on regional history, art, and culture. It curates other programs and events to delight more than 100,000 visitors each year.

7 Pacific Science Center

200 Second Ave. N., Seattle, WA 98109; 206-443-2001
pacificsciencecenter.org

You've got your Imax, your Laser Dome, your dinosaurs, your butterflies, your naked mole rats, and your interactive exhibits. Pacific Science Center has been keeping kids (and adults) engaged and curious since 1962.

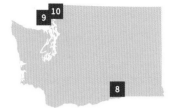

8 The REACH Museum

1943 Columbia Park Trail, Richland, WA 99353; 509-943-4100
visitthereach.org

Did someone say Ice Age floods? You won't find a stashed acorn, but you will learn about the often catastrophic geological history of Washington, as well as the state's recent past in the Mid-Columbia Basin.

9 The Whale Museum

62 First St. N., Friday Harbor, WA 98250; 360-378-4710
whalemuseum.org

Learn more about whale research and environmental dangers facing marine life, and review the map of recent sightings in the Salish Sea. Want to metaphorically adopt an orca? You can do that here.

10 Whatcom Museum

121 Prospect St., Bellingham, WA 98225; 360-778-8930
whatcommuseum.org

Art, nature, and Northwest history come together in this interactive museum experience.

Gingko Petrified Forest (see page 46) contains myriad geological delights, including plenty of petrified wood.

Asian Art Museum in Volunteer Park (see page 52)

HOUSING PERMANENT AND ROTATING EXHIBITIONS

from artists like Miwa Yanagi, Auguste Rodin, and the Chinatown Art Brigade collective, these museums capture culture and art from near and far, historical and contemporary.

GLOBAL MUSEUMS

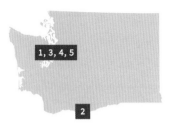

1 Asian Art Museum

1400 E. Prospect St., Seattle, WA 98112; 206-654-3210
seattleartmuseum.org/visit/asian-art-museum

It is easy to spend a whole day at this museum, which features a large collection of historical and contemporary Asian art in an impressive and newly renovated Art Deco building in the middle of expansive Volunteer Park.

2 Maryhill Museum of Art

35 Maryhill Museum Drive, Goldendale, WA 98620; 509-773-3733
maryhillmuseum.org

You'll be surprised by the views and what you'll find at this oddly located, oddly curated, mostly art museum that includes a Stonehenge Memorial for local servicemen who died in World War I.

3 National Nordic Museum

2655 NW Market St., Seattle, WA 98107; 206-789-5707
nordicmuseum.org

The museum shares Nordic culture through a gorgeous event and exhibition space in the traditionally Nordic neighborhood of Ballard.

4 Seattle Art Museum

1300 First Ave., Seattle, WA 98101; 206-654-3137
seattleartmuseum.org

Home to several permanent collections—and the iconic *Hammering Man*—SAM curates several high-profile fine art exhibits each year. The Olympic Sculpture Park and Asian Art Museum are both part of SAM.

5 Wing Luke Museum of the Asian Pacific American Experience

719 S. King St., Seattle, WA 98104; 206-623-5124
wingluke.org

Wing Luke is the only museum dedicated to sharing pan-Asian Pacific Americans' stories and experiences. Its Oral History Lab empowers community members to tell their own stories in their own voices.

Maryhill Museum of Art

Olympic Sculpture Park (see page 56) is a public waterfront park in Seattle.

THESE MUSEUMS SHOWCASE CONTEMPORARY ART

in beautiful spaces. Think sculpture, comics, film pieces, mixed media, painting, photography, and blown glass in beautifully curated exhibits. And that's just me thinking of what I've seen lately. You've got everything from crisp white walls to an outdoor sculpture park to choose from as the backdrop to your next Seattle-area contemporary museum adventure.

CONTEMPORARY MUSEUMS

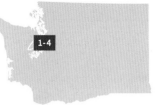

1-4

1 Bellevue Arts Museum

510 Bellevue Way NE, Bellevue, WA 98004; 425-519-0770
bellevuearts.org

Enjoy contemporary exhibitions, classes, tours, talks, films, and events for all ages at this museum in the heart of downtown Bellevue.

2 *Chihuly Garden and Glass*

305 Harrison St., Seattle, WA 98109; 206-753-4940
chihulygardenandglass.com

Featuring the works of contemporary glass artist Dale Chihuly, this long-term exhibition is a phenomenal place to bring your 6-year-old or your 6-year-old sense of wonder and joy, and have your mind blown while you puzzle over how the artist made the "what *is* that?" Located at the Seattle Center, the 1.5-acre exhibition space includes eight galleries, a 4,500-square-foot conservatory containing one of Chihuly's largest suspended sculptures, and a garden with four large-scale sculptures interspersed among the trees, flowers, and other plants.

3 The Frye

704 Terry Ave., Seattle, WA 98104; 206-622-9250
fryemuseum.org

A Seattle art museum dedicated to providing free access to art experiences and exhibitions by contemporary artists

4 Olympic Sculpture Park

2901 Western Ave., Seattle, WA 98121; 206-654-3100
seattleartmuseum.org/visit/olympic-sculpture-park

Part of the Seattle Art Museum, Olympic Sculpture Park is a free 9-acre area on the waterfront north of downtown Seattle that displays permanent and visiting sculptures. Sometimes, in nice weather, yoga classes are held in the park.

Contemporary Museums

Olympic Sculpture Park

The Toppenish Murals draw crowds in Eastern Washington.

THERE ARE MANY WAYS to experience the arts—through exhibitions, performances, festivals, and dance. This section lists many opportunities for art in Washington State. *See also Indigenous Peoples' Museums, page 95; Specialty Museums, page 41; Regional Museums, page 45; Global Museums, page 51; and Contemporary Museums, page 55.*

THE ARTS

Outdoor Murals

Henry Murals
Multiple locations, including Eighth Avenue Northwest and Northwest 45th Street, Seattle, WA 98107
itsahenry.com

SODO Track
Fifth Avenue South between Royal Brougham Way and Spokane Street, Seattle, WA 98134
sodotrack.com

Toppenish Murals
504 S. Elm St., Toppenish, WA 98948; 509-697-8995
visittoppenish.com

Theater

Anacortes Community Theatre
918 M Ave., Anacortes, WA 98221; 360-293-6829
acttheatre.com

Bellingham Theatre Guild
1600 H St., Bellingham, WA 98225; 360-733-1811
bellinghamtheatreguild.com

Edmonds Driftwood Players
The Wade James Theater, 950 Main St., Edmonds, WA 98020; 425-774-9600
edmondsdriftwoodplayers.org

Harlequin Productions
202 Fourth Ave. E., Olympia, WA 98501; 360-786-0151
harlequinproductions.org

(continued on next page)

Olympia Little Theatre
1925 Miller Ave. NE, Olympia, WA 98506; 360-786-9484
olympialittletheater.org

The Merc Playhouse
101 S. Glover St., Twisp, WA 98856; 509-997-7529
mercplayhouse.org

The Moore Theatre
1932 Second Ave., Seattle, WA 98101; 206-682-1414
stgpresents.org/moore

Regional Theatre of the Palouse
122 N. Grand Ave., Pullman, WA 99163; 509-334-0750
rtoptheatre.org

Paramount Theatre
911 Pine St., Seattle, WA 98101; 206-682-1414
stgpresents.org/paramount

Shakespeare in the Park
King and Snohomish Counties, WA; 206-748-1551
greenstage.org/shakespeare-in-the-park

Spokane Civic Theatre Main Stage
1020 N. Howard St., Spokane, WA 99201; 509-325-2507
spokanecivictheatre.com

Stage Left Theater
108 W. Third Ave., Spokane, WA 99201; 509-838-9727
spokanestageleft.org

Tacoma Little Theatre
210 N. I St., Tacoma, WA 98403; 253-272-2281
tacomalittletheatre.com

Theater Arts Guild
Lincoln Theatre, 712 S. First St., Mount Vernon, WA 98273; 360-770-1742
theaterartsguild.org

Theatre33
1632 116th Ave. NE, Bellevue, WA 98005; 425-633-0970
studio33wa.com/theatre33

Village Theatre
303 Front St. N., Issaquah, WA 98027; 425-392-2202
2710 Wetmore Ave., Everett, WA 98201; 425-257-8600
villagetheatre.org

Symphony

Auburn Symphony Orchestra
Auburn Performing Arts Center, 702 Fourth St. NE, Auburn, WA 98002; 253-887-7777
auburnsymphony.org

Northwest Symphony Orchestra
Highline Performing Arts Center, 401 S. 152nd St., Burien, WA 98148; 206-242-6321
northwestsymphonyorchestra.org

Olympia Symphony
Washington Center for the Performing Arts, 512 Washington St. SE, Olympia, WA 98501;
360-753-8586
olympiasymphony.org

Puget Sound Symphony Orchestra
Town Hall Seattle, 1119 Eighth Ave., Seattle, WA 98101; 206-652-4255
psso.org

Seattle Philharmonic Orchestra
Benaroya Hall, 200 University St., Seattle, WA 98101; 206-215-4800
seattlephil.org

Seattle Symphony
Benaroya Hall, 200 University St., Seattle, WA 98101; 866-833-4747
seattlesymphony.org

Spokane Symphony
Martin Woldson Theater at The Fox, 1001 W. Sprague Ave., Spokane, WA 99201;
509-624-1200
spokanesymphony.org

Symphony Tacoma
901 Broadway, Tacoma, WA 98402; 253-272-7264
symphonytacoma.org

Vancouver Symphony Orchestra
Skyview Concert Hall, 1300 NW 139th St., Vancouver, WA 98685; 360-735-7278
vancouversymphony.org

Walla Walla Symphony
Cordiner Hall, 46 S. Park St., Walla Walla, WA 99362; 509-529-8020
wwsymphony.org

Washington-Idaho Symphony
Gladish Community & Cultural Center, 115 NW State St., Ste. 116, Pullman, WA 99163;
208-874-4162
wa-idsymphony.org

Dance

Ballet Northwest
Washington Center for the Performing Arts, 512 Washington St. SE, Olympia, WA 98501;
360-943-8011
balletnorthwest.org

Bellingham Repertory Dance
Firehouse Performing Arts Center, 1314 Harris Ave., Bellingham, WA 98225; 360-734-2776
bhamrep.org

(continued on next page)

The Arts

Contra Dances
Bellingham, Darrington, Ellensburg, Lacey, Port Townsend, Tacoma, Vancouver, and Yakima
seattledance.org/contra

International Ballet Theatre
Meydenbauer Center, 11100 NE Sixth St., Bellevue, WA 98004; 425-284-0444
ibtbellevue.org

Olympic Ballet Theatre
Everett Performing Arts Center, 2710 Wetmore Ave., Everett, WA 98201; 425-257-8600
Edmonds Center for the Arts, 410 Fourth Ave. N., Edmonds, WA 98020; 425-774-7570
olympicballet.org

Pacific Northwest Ballet
McCaw Hall, 321 Mercer St., Seattle, WA 98109; 206-441-2424
pnb.org

Royal Scottish Country Dance Society—
Southwest Washington State Branch
Columbia Dance Center, 1700 Broadway St., Vancouver, WA 98663; 360-737-1922
vancouverusa-scd.org/events.html

Salsa Dances
Statewide
latindancecalendar.com/events/location/washington-state-usa

Salsa Dances
Various locations, Seattle
danceus.org/events/salsa/seattle-wa-salsa-calendar

Salsa and Swing Dancing at the Century Ballroom
915 E. Pine St., Seattle, WA 98122; 206-324-7263
centuryballroom.com/home/calendar

Spectrum Dance Theater
800 Lake Washington Blvd., Seattle, WA 98122; 206-325-4161
spectrumdance.org

Tacoma Belly Dance
Various locations, Tacoma, WA; 253-219-8870
tacomabellydance.com/shows

Velocity Dance Center
Seattle; 206-325-8773
velocitydancecenter.org/events

Vytal Movement Dance
Various locations, Spokane
vytalmovement.org

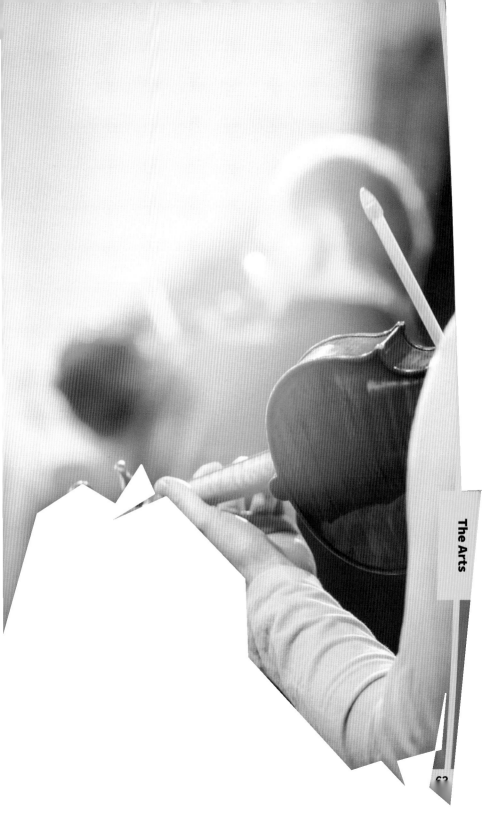

Manito Park, Spokane (see page 67)

WALKING AMONG CAREFULLY PLANTED PHLOX and freesia, flowering cacti and equidistant trees, you may think—as I do—of the people behind such orderly flora. There are those who designed the space, who planted the plants, who tended the garden over time. Plus, how many darling dogs have walked through here? Giant thanks to all the horticulturists, botanists, gardeners, and landscape magicians who contribute to conservatories, gardens, arboretums, and the like.

GARDENS, FLOWERS, AND ARBORETUMS

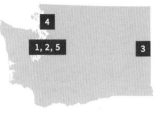

Bloedel Reserve

7571 NE Dolphin Drive, Bainbridge Island, WA 98110; 206-842-7631
bloedelreserve.org

The New York Times calls it "one of the country's most original and ambitious gardens." See for yourself. Two hours are recommended to stroll leisurely about the extensive grounds. There are gardens and arbors, pools and meadows. It feels like a true melding of manicured and natural landscapes. One moment there is a moss-covered forest floor, and the next, a raked Japanese garden.

The reserve was created by Prentice and Virginia Bloedel, philanthropists with roots in the timber industry who acquired the land on Bainbridge Island. Currently Bloedel Reserve's 14 distinct landscapes across the 150-acre property are open to the public. While you can enjoy the reserve anytime during its open hours, it also offers seasonal events, including walks with horticultural experts.

Kubota Gardens

9817 55th Ave. S., Seattle, WA 98118; 206-725-5060
kubotagarden.org; seattle.gov/parks/find/parks/kubota-garden

When Fujitaro Kubota bought several acres of swamp in Rainier Beach in 1927, he knew how beautiful he could make it. With a dream to bring Japanese gardening techniques to the Northwest (and its native plants), Kubota—entirely self-taught as a gardener—started a gardening company. He designed and created gardens throughout the Greater Seattle area, including the Japanese garden at Bloedel Reserve and the gardens on Seattle University's campus. His 5-acre personal garden, which served as an area to perfect techniques and maintain a nursery for his business, soon grew to include 20 acres.

During World War II, the Kubota family was forcibly relocated and interned at Camp Minidoka in Idaho. The garden was left vacant. Upon the family's return, Kubota and his sons rebuilt the family business—and continued to add features to the garden. Today there are bridges, rock walls, waterfalls, and ponds. There is stonework and trails and few views of the neighborhood outside. Its own oasis (and a designated historical landmark), Kubota Gardens is now run by the City of Seattle. Enjoy it on your own, or book a guided tour (for groups of 7 or more).

3 Rose Hill, Manito Park

1702 S. Grand Blvd., Spokane, WA 99203; 509-625-6200
my.spokanecity.org/parks/gardens/rose-hill

The Rose Hill section of Manito Park in Spokane contains over 150 types of roses, including native species and hybrids. Rose Hill is maintained by the Spokane Rose Society in conjunction with Spokane Parks and Recreation. It was named the nation's best rose garden by All-America Rose Selections in 2007. Beyond Rose Hill, there are the Lilac Garden, Duncan Garden, Ferris Garden, and Nishinomiya Tsutakawa Japanese Garden. These distinct areas, along with the Mirror Pond and Gaiser Conservatory, make Manito a worthwhile place to enjoy many types of gardens.

4 Skagit Valley Tulip Festival

311 W. Kincaid St., Mount Vernon, WA 98273
tulipfestival.org

April is tulip month in Skagit Valley. The Tulip Festival hosts events and visitors April 1–30. The tulips will bloom when they bloom, but there is usually a variety blooming all month long, and fields with daffodils as well. And what a sight to see the bright colors for miles and miles! There are guided tours, or you can make your own way to Mount Vernon and pick a stop on the map to start. You'll want to travel by car or bicycle, as the farms can be miles apart from one another. You may choose just one or two places to stop, or check out several on your trip. There are also affiliated art shows and galleries if you need a break from the fields (or the weather).

5 The Spheres

2111 Seventh Ave., Seattle, WA 98121; 360-428-5959
seattlespheres.com

Primarily a place for Amazon employees to meet and ideate closer to nature, the Spheres are spherical glass conservatories open to the public on some weekend days each month. Make a reservation in advance to secure a viewing time. With more than 40,000 plants from the cloud forest regions of over 30 countries, The Spheres are packed full of greenery from the floor to the four-story ceiling to the vertical living walls. The domes need to be kept at precise temperatures and humidity levels to allow the plant life to thrive. In addition to all the green, you'll

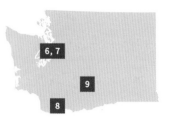

spot pops of color in leaves and flowers. There are staircases, elevators, ramps, and skyways to all the levels and little nooks where you
can sit and take it all in.

6 Volunteer Park Conservatory

1400 E. Galer St., Seattle, WA 98112; 206-684-4743
volunteerparkconservatory.org

For a small admission fee ($4 as I write this), you can visit the
Volunteer Park Conservatory in Seattle. It hosts a number of
workshops and events—I'm bummed I just missed the Cactus &
Succulents class. Since its opening in 1912, there have been a couple
of major renovations. As you walk through the space, you'll see
tropical and subtropical plants, including orchids, bromeliads, and
palms, carnivorous plants, and cacti—some plants in the collection
are over 75 years old. There is a gift shop on-site, and they usually
have some plants for sale. The Conservatory does a couple of large
plant sales each year as well. Look for them in the spring and fall.

7 Washington Park Arboretum and UW Botanic Gardens

2300 Arboretum Dr. E., Seattle, WA 98112; 206-543-8800
botanicgardens.uw.edu/washington-park-arboretum; seattlejapanesegarden.org

The Washington Park Arboretum and UW Botanic Gardens are free
and open to the public (with the exception of the Seattle Japanese
Garden, which requires an admission fee). The 230 acres encom-
pass natural areas and a variety of gardens, including the Pacific
Connections Garden, the Woodland Garden, the Rhododendron
Glen, and others.

If you start your trip at the Graham Visitors Center, you can pick up
a map to help identify trails and distinct areas of the park. Tours are
available, or feel free to explore on your own. You may find yourself
on the marshy shoreline boardwalk looking out at Foster and Marsh
Islands or strolling along Azalea Way admiring the spring blooms.

8 Wind River Arboretum

1262 Hemlock Road, Carson, WA 98610; 509-427-3200
fs.usda.gov/pnw/experimental-forests-and-ranges/wind-river-experimental-forest

In 1909 research began at Wind River Experimental Forest, which was formally established a few years later. The forest includes the Wind River Arboretum—the Northwest's oldest. Trees and plant cuttings were transplanted here from vastly different climates to evaluate their performance, lifespan, and resistance or susceptibility to the local environment alongside native species. Spoiler alert: The local species found in old-growth forests—like cedars, hemlocks, and firs—grow best in the Pacific Northwest. Many of the hardwoods and subtropical trees have since died. Studies here have helped show that investment should be made in growing and harvesting local species for forestry work. The research, for example, on Douglas firs helped provide critical information for their success in plantation growth and the best management practices for similar forests. The Wind River Arboretum is much different from a well-maintained, pruned arboretum. You can walk the footsteps of more than 100 years of research and see trees that are around 400 years old. There is much to be learned.

9 Yakima Area Arboretum

1401 Arboretum Drive, Yakima, WA 98901; 509-248-7337
ahtrees.org

Located along the Yakima River's riparian corridor, this 46-acre wetland-turned-farmland-turned-arboretum has cultivated gardens, natural areas, and a diverse collection of trees. The arboretum also offers classes and events, from mushroom identification to beginner bonsai workshops, and an interpretive center and gift shop are located on-site. Bonus: If you love cacti, there is a large collection at the Hillside Desert Botanical Gardens about 6 miles south in Union Gap. The Yakima Area Arboretum is free and open to the public.

The Skagit Valley Tulip Festival takes place in April.

WASHINGTON STATE TAKES A LOT OF PRIDE in its agriculture. Find farms where you can pick berries or apples, corn mazes, and pumpkin patches here. Visit Skagit Valley during the tulip festival, and choose some bulbs to plant in your own front yard. Looking for something more adult? Wander through hops, taste samples at breweries and wineries, or bicycle along a three-stop, 10-mile cider route.

ORCHARDS, FARMS, AND VINEYARDS

Orchards and Farms

Bellewood Farms
6140 Guide Meridian Road, Lynden, WA 98264; 360-318-7720
bellewoodfarms.com

Bob's Corn & Pumpkin Farm
10917 Elliott Road, Snohomish, WA 98296; 360-668-2506
bobscorn.com

Green Bluff Farms
Multiple farms in Green Bluff, WA 99021
greenbluffgrowers.com

Jones Creek Farms
32260 Burrese Road, Sedro-Woolley, WA 98284
skagitvalleyfruit.com

Jubilee Farm
229 W. Snoqualmie River Road NE, Carnation, WA 98014; 425-240-4929
jubileefarm.org

Skagit Valley Tulips
311 W. Kincaid St., Mount Vernon, WA 98273; 360-428-5959
tulipfestival.org

U-Pick Farms

Bill's Berry Farm
3674 N. County Line Road, Grandview, WA 98930; 509-882-3200
billsberryfarm.com

Bolles Organic Berry Farm
17930 Tualco Loop Road, Monroe, WA 98272; 360-805-1980
facebook.com/bollesorganic

(continued on next page)

Pigmans Produce
10633 Steilacoom Road SE, Olympia, WA 98513; 360-491-3276
pigmansproduce.com

Schuh Farms
15565 WA 536, Mount Vernon, WA 98273; 360-424-6982
facebook.com/schuh-farms-286087151435556

The Stutzman Ranch
2226 Easy St., Wenatchee, WA 98801; 509-669-3276
thestutzmanranch.com

Beer, Wine, and Spirits Tours

Bale Breaker Brewing Company
1801 Birchfield Road, Yakima, WA 98901; 509-424-4000
balebreaker.com

Barnard Griffin Vineyard
878 Tulip Lane, Richland, WA 99352; 509-627-0266
barnardgriffin.com

Chateau Ste. Michelle
14111 NE 145th St., Woodinville, WA 98072; 425-488-1133
ste-michelle.com

Copperworks Distilling Company
1250 Alaskan Way, Seattle, WA 98101; 206-504-7604
copperworksdistilling.com

Gallagher's Where-U-Brew
180 W. Dayton St.,. #105, Edmonds, WA 98020; 425-776-4209
whereubrew.com

Olympic Peninsula Cider Route
Multiple orchards, including Finnriver, 124 Center Road, Chimacum, WA 98325;
360-339-8478
olympicculinaryloop.com/taste-trail-cider-route

Beer hops used by craft brewers, on the vine, growing in the sun, and almost ready for harvest

An American oystercatcher at Dungeness National Wildlife Refuge (see page 76)

SHOREBIRDS, FLYCATCHERS, PELICANS, loons, and eagles are just some of the birds that make a home for themselves in Washington State. Whether you are new to birding, or have been at it for years, grab your notebook, your field guide, your binoculars, and your camera: The parks, rainforests, shores, reserves, and refuges are brimming with life. If you're not normally one to go bird-watching, consider listening for birdsong on your next hike. Even if you don't know their names, take note of something about them that strikes you. Good luck out there.

BIRD-WATCHING SPOTS

1 Billy Frank Jr. Nisqually National Wildlife Refuge

100 Brown Farm Road NE, Olympia, WA 98516; 360-753-9467
fws.gov/refuge/billy_frank_jr_nisqually

The Nisqually River Delta is home to many resident and migratory birds. In 1974 the Billy Frank Jr. Nisqually National Wildlife Refuge was established by the U.S. Fish & Wildlife Service (FWS) to protect this habitat. One incredible event to watch is the chum salmon run from December to mid-January. It's not the salmon you'll be watching but the dozens of bald eagles with 7-foot wingspans that may be out fishing. The FWS has a bird list for the refuge available at its website so you can keep track of what you spot. You may see peregrine falcons, great horned owls, sandpipers, and shrikes. Nest sites of nearly 100 species have been recorded on the Nisqually Delta. The refuge includes an extensive estuary boardwalk that extends across the mudflats, providing excellent views. Don't forget your binoculars.

2 Dungeness National Wildlife Refuge

554 Voice of America Road W., Sequim, WA 98382; 360-457-8451
fws.gov/refuge/dungeness

Dungeness National Wildlife Refuge was specifically established to protect and conserve the area for migratory birds. Snowy owls, seabirds, and shorebirds can all be found here. You may spot some harbor seals too. But if it's birds you're looking for, birds you will find. There is a large population of brant here that feed on eelgrass. Depending on the time of your visit, you could come across oystercatchers, dunlins, and least sandpipers. On my last visit, pigeon guillemots were nesting in the cliffs, just after the leisurely 0.5-mile descent from the trailhead. Rather than walking out on the spit, turn left and look up at the cliffs (and in the waters by the shore). Once you do walk out on the 5-mile spit, look for birds along the shoreline, in the water, and perched on driftwood.

3 Grays Harbor National Wildlife Refuge

1131 Airport Way, Hoquiam, WA, 98550; 360-753-9467
fws.gov/refuge/grays_harbor; shorebirdfestival.com

Home to the Shorebird Festival, Grays Harbor National Wildlife Refuge is an excellent place for birding. The shorebird migration north takes place in late April and early May. Many species of shorebirds stop at Grays Harbor on their way to the Arctic, some clocking up to 15,000 miles for their round-trip journey, according to the Shorebird Festival website. The best viewing times are within 2 hours of high tide. For a viewing schedule, see the U.S. Fish & Wildlife Service website. The refuge has a boardwalk and trails, and bird- and wildlife-viewing are popular year-round.

4 Little Pend Oreille National Wildlife Refuge

1230 Bear Creek Road, Colville, WA 99144; 509-684-8384
fws.gov/refuge/little_pend_oreille; wabirder.com/docs/PendOreille_list.pdf

When you visit the Little Pend Oreille National Wildlife Refuge, you'll learn that the U.S. Fish & Wildlife Service established the refuge in 1939 with the goal of protecting and conserving this habitat and breeding ground for migratory birds and other animals. Over 206 species of birds, as well as lynx, bobcats, cougars, bears, moose, and elk, live here (among many other animals). At over 40,000 acres, it is huge. The refuge is part of the Selkirk Mountains, situated between the Rockies and the Cascades. The area has a great variety of habitat—a mixed-conifer forest, mountains, marsh, meadow, lakes, ponds, and streams. This provides a great deal of species with homes, both temporary and permanent.

White-headed, black-backed, and three-toed woodpeckers; great gray owls; ospreys; wild turkeys; western bluebirds; and black-chinned hummingbirds can all be found here. See the list from Washington Birder to keep track of what you spot (or hear).

5 Mount Rainier National Park

39000 WA 706 E., Ashford, WA 98304; 360-569-2211
nps.gov/mora/learn/nature/birds.htm; tinyurl.com/mtranierbirdchecklist

Mount Rainier National Park has rivers, lakes, marshes, alpine and subalpine areas, and forests and meadows. There is many a home to be made for birds and other wildlife. Different species live in different regions of the park, so depending on the time of your visit and what you're hoping to spot, you can choose an area (or elevation) accordingly. You may see northern spotted owls, barred owls, peregrine

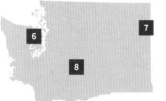

falcons, red-tailed hawks, harlequin ducks, and many kinds of warblers and finches. There are too many species to list here, so check out the bird checklist from the National Park Service to keep track of your findings and have a better idea of what might be common (or rare) to see in the current season.

6 Olympic National Park

3002 Mount Angeles Road, Port Angeles, WA 98362; 360-565-3130
nps.gov/olym/planyourvisit/birdwatching-in-olympic.htm;
audubon.org/climate/national-parks/olympic-national-park

With Pacific Ocean coastline, rainforest, mountains, rivers, and lakes, Olympic National Park has a rich diversity of bird species across its many distinct habitats. Some favorites include the red-breasted sapsucker, the bufflehead, the belted kingfisher, and the northern pygmy owl. But you have your own favorites. I've included the link to the National Audubon Society's assessment of which species might be in the park now, based on the season, this year's climate, and other factors. Over 250 species inhabit the park throughout the year. I hope you see some beauties.

7 Palouse to Pines Loop: The Great Washington State Birding Trail

Eastern Washington
wa.audubon.org/birds/great-washington-state-birding-trail-app;
tinyurl.com/palousetopinesbooklet

The Great Washington State Birding Trail accounts for birding locations across the entirety of Washington State (some of which overlap with my earlier entries). That said, I couldn't talk about birding without a shout-out to the Washington Audubon Society and their work. They produce maps of different areas of the birding trail, including the Cascade Loop, Palouse to Pines Loop, Sun and Sage Loop, Coulee Corridor, Puget Loop, Southwest Loop, and the Olympic Loop. If you prefer to go digital, see the link to the app above.

The Palouse to Pines Loop, as an example, gives you the opportunity to see some 215 species of year-round and migratory birds that may perch in 51 of the included spots in the Inland Northwest. The pamphlet includes maps and descriptions of habitats of interest. While there is artwork of birds (like western tanagers, Cassin's vireo, and loggerhead shrike), the booklets aren't true replacements for field guides with images and descriptions of the bird species themselves. That said, they are very thorough in providing lists of which species you'll see in which areas. Going to Calispell Lake, driving over Sherman Pass Overlook, or camping at Mount Spokane State Park? The "Palouse to Pines" booklet will be a very helpful guide for the birding component of your adventure.

8 Wenas Wildlife Area

29360 N. Wenas Road, Selah, WA 98942; 509-697-4503
wdfw.wa.gov/places-to-go/wildlife-areas/wenas-wildlife-area;
bentler.us/eastern-washington/animals/birds/default.aspx

Home of the Washington Audubon Society's annual Memorial Day weekend gathering, Wenas Wildlife Area is a premier spot for bird-watching. You may see mountain and western bluebirds, calliope hummingbirds, white-headed woodpeckers, and MacGillivray's warblers. If you're on the lookout for larger animal life, you may come across mule deer, bighorn sheep, and elk during your travels. There are several spots to amble around, including Umtanum Canyon, Umtanum Ridge, and Yakima Rim Skyline Trail. The Wenas Wildlife Area encompasses nearly 105,000 acres. The forest, the lush banks of Wenas Creek, the shrub-steppe area of the desert, and the basalt flats each contribute to the birds found here. Please let me know if you see a flammulated owl. "Flammies" are tiny for owls—weighing in around 50–65 grams (1.8–2.3 ounces)—with a wingspan of a little over a foot. Listen for a series of somewhat deep single or double hoots.

Site of the Glines Canyon Dam Removal on the Elwha River, Port Angeles (see page 83)

THIS THEME INCLUDES PLACES that highlight, protect, preserve, or showcase the environment or its inhabitants in one way or another. There's the greenest building, a hillside–turned–food forest, an actual rainforest, and a wallaby farm, to name a few. Whether you like to be out in nature or see it from the comfort of a tree house window, you'll find a place to visit in this section.

ENVIRONMENTAL TOURISM

3

4

1, 2

Environmental
Tourism

1 Beacon Food Forest

Fifteenth Avenue South at South Dakota Street, Seattle, WA 98108
beaconfoodforest.org

A gardening technique after my own heart, the food forest is situated on 7 acres of land in the Beacon Hill neighborhood of Seattle. The site expands down the side of the hill and features fruit and nut trees, berry bushes, and other edible plants. Using a combination of native plant reforestation and permaculture practices to grow food, Beacon Food Forest aims to bring Seattle's diverse community together around food and stewardship.

As I write this, the food forest is a work in progress. It began in 2009 as a design, and Phase I of the plan is complete. Currently, 1.75 acres of food forest are up and running—growing and producing. You can visit or join a work party to become a part of the magic. The full acreage will include more food forest, educational spaces, and a community "P-Patch" garden (part of a city Department of Neighborhoods program), where community members can grow their own food. The staff can also provide advice and support if you're looking to build your own food forest. There's an idea . . .

2 Bullitt Center

1501 E. Madison St., Seattle, WA 98122
bullittcenter.org/home/tour; millerhull.com/project/bullitt-center

The Bullitt Center opened its doors on Earth Day in 2013. Part of the Living Building Challenge (2.0), it combined ideas and innovations from around the globe to create a beautifully designed 52,000-square-foot office space that could produce its own energy, capture and treat its own water, and use materials without toxins—the first and largest commercial building to do so. Part of the beauty of the building is its relationship to the outdoors, from the locally sourced Douglas fir to the views out of the 10-foot-tall windows. Tours are by reservation only.

82

3 Cape Flattery, Olympic Coast National Marine Sanctuary

GPS Coordinates: N48° 23.094' W124° 42.946' (Cape Loop Road, Neah Bay, WA 98357)
makah.com/activities/cape-flattery-trail

Talk about isolation . . . wow. Windblown sitka spruces dot the shore where big rock outcrops creep into the deep blue waters. From here you can see the Cape Flattery Lighthouse out on Tatoosh Island in the distance. Cape Flattery is the northwesternmost point in the contiguous United States and is part of the Makah Reservation (see Makah Cultural and Research Center, page 103). This boundary, where the Strait of Juan de Fuca meets the Pacific, is also the northern border of the Olympic Coast National Marine Sanctuary.

Overseen by the National Oceanic and Atmospheric Administration, the sanctuary works to protect natural and cultural resources across 3,188 square miles of marine waters. Many species—including sea lions, sea otters, orca and gray whales, migratory shorebirds, sea urchins, and fish—call this place home. Stop by the Olympic Coast Discovery Center to learn more.

4 Glines Canyon Dam Removal Site

GPS Coordinates: N48° 02.511' W123° 35.303' (Olympic Hot Springs Road,
Port Angeles, WA 98363; 360-565-3130
nps.gov/olym/learn/nature/dam-removal.htm; nps.gov/olym/learn/nature
/elwha-ecosystem-restoration.htm; nps.gov/olym/learn/nature/upload
/ElwhaRiverRestorationBrochure_2012-3.pdf

For thousands of years, the Elwha River supplied the Lower Elwha Klallam tribe with a way of life. Salmon and trout ran the river, and many species found a home here. The river was the beating heart of the ecosystem. With the timber industry that helped supply America's growth, several landscapes were forcibly changed. Two dams—Elwha and Glines Canyon—went up on the Elwha in the early 1900s, blocking the salmon migration and flooding the lands. It was 100 years before the mistake was corrected.

The Elwha became the largest dam-removal project in the United States. It took decades to plan and half a year to complete. After the Elwha came down, Glines Canyon Dam was removed in 2014, freeing the river. The Elwha River Restoration has allowed an ecosystem that depended on the river's uninterrupted flow to begin to heal. Now scientists have the opportunity to study how this impacts the habitat, including the salmon population. There are several places to visit the Elwha (see link to brochure). At the time of writing this guide, Madison Falls Trailhead provides the best access to hike in to the Glines Canyon

Spillway Overlook or the Overlook at Whiskey Bend. On your way, stop in at any Olympic National Park visitor center to learn more. The impact of dam removal will be felt for generations to come.

5 Hall of Mosses

18113 Upper Hoh Road, Forks, WA 98331; 360-565-2985 or 360-565-3130
nps.gov/olym/planyourvisit/visiting-the-hoh.htm

The shaded, moist forest floor of the Olympic Peninsula is an ideal home for moss. There are many kinds of mosses, but what I love about them is how fluffy and green they are. Even on a rainy winter day, the moss makes me smile. On my earliest hikes on the west side of Washington State, something always seemed fairy tale–like, with the enormity of the trees and the moss-draped branches.

Mosses play an important role in the rainforest. They help prevent erosion by preserving the soil surface, and they help hold water to keep the area moist for other plants. If you, too, admire mosses, go on this short hike in Olympic National Park. It won't disappoint.

6 Northwest Trek Wildlife Park

11610 Trek Drive E., Eatonville, WA 98328; 360-832-6117
nwtrek.org

Focusing on conservation and education, the Northwest Trek Wildlife Park provides an opportunity to see and discover Northwestern wildlife and habitat. Several tours and exhibits allow you to build your own adventure. You can tour the park by tram, on foot, or in a jeep. If you want to hear elk bugling, visit during the rutting season (September–October).

Both free-roaming and contained habitats are maintained for the animals (depending on the species). There's an even longer roster, but the park includes cougars, moose, elk, owls, wolves, bears, beavers, otters, porcupines, and banana slugs. If you are looking to be a part of Northwest Trek as more than a visitor, the park is always looking for volunteers.

7 Seattle's Giant Sequoia Tree

Fourth Avenue and Stewart Street, Seattle, WA 98181

If you've been to Seattle, you may have walked right by this tree. But you also may have stopped in your tracks to admire it. It's smack in the middle of downtown's shopping core by Westlake Center at the intersection of Fourth Avenue, Stewart Street, and Olive Way. Each November the tree gets dressed up in lights, but all year it stands an impressive 80 feet tall. It used to be even taller, but a storm damaged some of the tree. In fact, a lot of things are working against it—like the pavement impeding its root system, and the car exhaust. Seattle Department of Transportation's Urban Forestry program takes measures to help by aerating the soil and adding compost.

This tree wasn't always here. It's hard to believe, but this giant sequoia was transplanted in 1973 from a location on Aurora Avenue. It has its stories (like the time #ManInTree was up there for over 24 hours in 2016). The giant sequoia certainly makes me think of a time before all these buildings were here, when trees were the only things standing this tall. It makes me want to visit the forests outside the city. There's another giant sequoia a few miles away in Leschi Park, but this one at Westlake looks particularly remarkable because of the stark contrast with its neighboring buildings.

8 TreeHouse Point

6922 Preston-Fall City Road SE, Issaquah, WA 98027; 425-441-8087
treehousepoint.com

Six tree houses. In the forest. For adults. I don't know about you, but I love a tree house. I climbed many a tree in my youth (and spent a lot of hours sitting in an oak—at least I think it was an oak—in my yard), but I've never had a proper tree house. I grew up hearing stories about how my mom and aunt would hang out in their tree house, which my grandfather had outfitted with electricity and a phone line. What? Jealous!

The tree houses at TreeHouse Point are available as overnight lodging or simply to admire on a tour of the property (by appointment only). They have electricity and heat, and each features a slightly different design. On one, it's the windows that wow (I'm looking at you, Trillium). On another, it could be the bridge, the staircase, the chandelier, or the fact that it's two stories that delights you. Yes, these are little gems in the forest. Tours last about an hour and happen rain or shine.

9 Wallaby Ranch

35303 SE Fish Hatchery Road, Fall City, WA 98024; 206-354-8624
wallabyranch.org

Rex and Tawny Paperd's one pet wallaby turned into, well, many.
They converted their 10 acres into the Wallaby Ranch, home to gray
and albino Bennett's wallabies, wallaroos, and red kangaroos. In
addition to being USDA-licensed breeders, they also run educational
programming at local schools and host small groups for tours at the
ranch (by reservation only). Tours last 1–1.5 hours and include meeting the mob—that's actually what you call a group of wallabies
or kangaroos. If you're lucky, you'll get a smooch from a joey or see
a wee one in its mother's pouch.

10 Wenatchee River Institute

347 Division St., Leavenworth, WA 98826; 509-548-0181
wenatcheeriverinstitute.org

The Wenatchee River Institute (WRI) provides environmental learning opportunities with the goal of "connecting people, community,
and the natural world." The 9-acre nature preserve sits along the
Wenatchee River not far from Leavenworth.

WRI hosts camps for youth, as well as all-ages workshops, like
Fundamentals of Wildlife Tracking and Fly Tying. Salmon Walks,
Mushroom Forages, Bird Fest, and other hands-on activities are
held throughout the year. The Red Barn Learning Center at the
Barn Beach Reserve is where film screenings and discussions
are held, including talks on Sustainability and the Science on Tap!
lecture series.

Because WRI is a hands-on learning center, the staff leads "field
trips" to explore, learn about, and admire the natural world. The
institute also has an on-site garden where folks from the community
can grow food. Check the calendar and choose a time to enjoy a
walk, take an adventure, or learn from the experts and scientists
who bring these programs to life.

The ever-enchanting Hall of Mosses in Hoh Rain Forest, Olympic National Park (see page 84)

Salmon Bake at Tillicum Village (see page 93)

INDIGENOUS PEOPLES have a vibrant and diverse history in Washington State, evidence of which dates back over 10,000 years. And they are still here. Northwest tribes continue to evolve while sustaining culture, language, arts, and community for future generations. Tribal investment in education, environmental protection, museums, and cultural centers is just part of the story. One event that brings many people together to celebrate, to practice traditional lifeways, and to share stories, dancing, meals, and song is the annual canoe journey. *See also Indigenous Peoples' Museums, page 93.*

INDIGENOUS PEOPLES' CULTURE

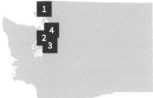

1 Canoe Journey

tribaljourneys.wordpress.com; facebook.com/officialtribaljourneys

The intertribal Canoe Journey has been happening annually since 1989—the year of Washington's state centennial. It is meant to bring tribes together to celebrate traditional arts, culture, and lifeways; to share language and song; and to honor the connection to the land, to the water, and to each other. The journey changes from year to year, with different nations hosting. Canoe families paddle for several days (or weeks), stopping each night. Each year the nations work together to create a map that approximates arrival dates and locations where tribes will host canoes along the way. The paddle culminates in Protocol at the host tribe's location, where boats ask permission to come ashore and participate in a multiday celebration of meals, dancing, drumming, and sharing stories and cultural heritage. Indigenous people throughout the area are invited to participate in the paddle; some come from as far as Hawaii and Alaska. Everyone is welcome to gather to watch the canoes land.

The event grows each year—approximately 10,000 participants and 100 canoes paddled to Lummi in 2019. These are subject to change, but the next several years of the canoe journey already have committed hosts. You may have to do a little research to confirm the dates of the journey. The hosting tribe extends a formal invitation and typically creates a website (and Facebook group) with more information.

2022: Paddle to Muckleshoot

2023: Paddle to Celilo, Warm Springs, Oregon

2024: Paddle to Suquamish Tribe

2025: Paddle to Lower Elwha

2 Chief Seattle Days

Downtown Suquamish, WA 98392
suquamish.nsn.us

Established in 1911, this festival celebrates Chief Seattle, namesake of the largest city in Washington, with canoe races, a salmon bake, sports, drumming, dancing, and a parade. Each year a memorial is held at the chief's grave site to recognize his accomplishments and honor the sacrifices he made for the Suquamish people. More events have been added over the years, including a powwow, a fun run, craft and food vendors, and a royalty pageant. The multiday event takes place in mid-August. (See also the Suquamish Museum, page 97.)

3 Duwamish Longhouse & Cultural Center

4705 W. Marginal Way SW, Seattle, WA 98106; 206-431-1582
duwamishtribe.org/longhouse; facebook.com/duwamishculturalcenter

Chief Si'ahl, Seattle's namesake, was Duwamish on his mother's side (his father was Suquamish). He became an important leader of six Puget Sound tribes, and his was the first name listed on the Treaty of Point Elliott, signed in 1855. Seattle (and beyond) is the ancestral land of the Duwamish people.

Because the Duwamish are the first people of Seattle, it is only fitting that the Duwamish Longhouse & Cultural Center (DLCC), which opened its doors in 2009, is located here, on the Duwamish River. It's very close to Duwamish Site No. 1, an important archaeological site discovered in 1975, some artifacts from which are on display at the longhouse. DLCC has a free museum and art gallery, and the space is used for both private and public events. Review the events calendar on its website; it hosts many workshops and other recurring events.

4 Hibulb Cultural Center & Natural History Preserve

6410 23rd Ave. NE, Tulalip, WA 98271; 360-716-2600
hibulbculturalcenter.org

The Tulalip people's culture and heritage can be seen throughout the Hibulb Cultural Center. Open since 2011, the HCC offers tours where, according to its website, you can "experience the journey of the Tulalip people. You will learn about our traditional territories, the importance of the cedar trees, our seven value stories, and seasonal lifeways." There are rotating and permanent exhibits that include archaeological artifacts, art, family trees, and a wall to honor Tulalip veterans. The center also has a gift shop, a research library, and a longhouse, plus

50 acres of forest and wetlands. Several events take place here,· including an annual film festival; weaving gatherings and other workshops; and poetry, film, lecture, and culture series. Review the events calendar on its website for details.

5 Makah Days

Downtown Neah Bay, WA 98357
makah.com/activities/makah-days

One year when I was out on the coast visiting Shi Shi beach (on Makah land), I happened to be in town for Makah Days. My favorite part was the canoe racing—not just for the beautiful boats but also for the camaraderie and cheering from the folks on land. The event takes place over a weekend in late August (near the anniversary of the first US flag raising on Makah land, in 1913) and is a chance to get together to celebrate thousands of years of Makah culture, as well as the anniversary of the Makah people's becoming US citizens and their contributions to the country. So much happens that weekend—a talent show, a street fair, traditional canoe racing, a parade, dancing, *slahal* games, softball, fireworks, and the coronation of the Makah Royal Court. Neighboring tribes often join for the fun and to share stories and culture. (Also see the Makah Cultural and Research Center, page 103.)

6 Quileute Days

Downtown La Push, WA 98350
quileutenation.org

Quileute heritage and modern culture are highlighted in the community over the course of Quileute Days (usually in mid-July each year). The Quileute tribe celebrates together with canoe races, stick games, a salmon bake, softball, traditional singing and dancing, and a big parade. The royalty pageant takes place on Friday, and events continue through Sunday. If you think you know something about the Quileute people from *Twilight,* you'd be better off visiting yourself to learn about their true history and traditions.

7 Salmon Bake, Tillicum Village

Blake Island, Port Orchard, WA 98366; 888-623-1445
argosycruises.com/argosy-cruises/tillicum-excursion

Argosy Cruises hosts a 4-hour excursion to Tillicum Village on Blake Island. Visitors are invited into the Tillicum longhouse, where Coast Salish totems are on display and where visitors can enjoy a meal featuring salmon baked in the traditional method around an open fire pit, as well as shared dances and history of Pacific Northwest Coastal tribes. Tillicum Village was founded in 1962 by Bill Hewitt, who was not native but whose personal mission included sharing and promoting the culture and history of Indigenous people.

Tillicum Village was purchased from the Hewitt family by Argosy Cruises in 2009. While Argosy employs several Indigenous people and relies on their capacity as advisors, know that this is not a typical longhouse that belongs to an Indigenous community. Rather, several cultures from the Pacific Northwest coastal community are represented here in the art, performances, and storytelling. Some families have participated at Tillicum Village for generations—as carvers, singers, drummers, and dancers—sharing the multiple histories of this land and neighboring lands as far away as British Columbia.

8 Yakama Nation Treaty Day

100 Spiel-yi Loop, Toppenish, WA 98948; 509-865-2800 (Yakama Nation Cultural Center)
yakamamuseum.com; tinyurl.com/yakamanationevents

In early June each year, members of the Confederated Tribes and Bands of the Yakama Nation and the greater community gather together to celebrate Treaty Day and the anniversary of the Yakama Nation Cultural Center. The anniversary of the June 9, 1855, signing of the Yakama Nation Treaty is an opportunity to celebrate US citizenship and the continued protection of Yakama rights to land, water, and traditional ways of life, including hunting and gathering. There's a lot of fun events to enjoy—usually over an entire week—such as artisan and food vendors, a powwow, a flag raising, stick games, softball tournaments, a rodeo, and a parade. (See also Yakama National Museum & Cultural Center, page 97, and the Toppenish Murals, page 59.)

Quileute totem pole in the town of La Push

INDIGENOUS PEOPLE have a long and rich history in what is now called Washington State. A deep intergenerational connection to this land has been forged over thousands of years. Indigenous peoples' history, culture, specialty handicrafts, and other art are on display in many museums and cultural centers in Washington. In these Washington State tribal museums, Indigenous art, history, and culture are at the forefront. *See also Indigenous Peoples' Culture, page 89.*

INDIGENOUS PEOPLES' MUSEUMS

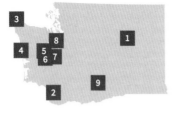

1 Colville Tribal Museum

512 Mead Way, Coulee Dam, WA 99116; 509-633-0751
colvilletribes.com/colville-tribal-museum

Learn about local history from the Confederated Tribes of the Colville Reservation in this thoughtfully designed museum. Unique gifts are available in the shop.

2 Lelooska Foundation & Cultural Center

165 Merwin Village Road, Ariel, WA 98603; 360-225-9522
lelooska.org

This living history museum provides the chance to learn about the stories and culture of the Kwakwaka'wakw (Kwakiutl) people and Northwest Coast First Nations people through dance, song, and storytelling.

3 Makah Museum

1880 Bayview Ave., Neah Bay, WA 98357; 360-645-2711
makahmuseum.com

Beautiful exhibits and hugely significant cultural artifacts make this museum worth the drive to a remote and stunning corner of the state. See also Makah Cultural and Research Center, page 103.

4 Quinault Tribal Museum

807 Fifth Ave., Suite 1, Taholah, WA; 360-276-8215 ext. 245
graysharbormuseums.org/quinault-tribal-museum
quinaultindiannation.com

A display of artifacts, historic documents, and a library collection reside on-site at the museum.

5 Skokomish Tribal Museum

80 N. Tribal Center Road, Skokomish Nation, WA 98584; 360-426-4232 ext. 2015
skokomish.org/cultural-resources

Carrying on the values, traditions, stories, and language of the Twana people, the museum houses many artifacts, including carvings, baskets, and paintings.

6 Squaxin Island Tribe Museum Library and Research Center

150 SE Kwuh-Deegs-Altxw, Shelton, WA 98584; 360-432-3839
squaxinislandmuseum.org

Walk into the Hall of the Seven Inlets to see huge, colorful depictions of watersheds and their stories. The museum exhibits art in many forms, including sacred belongings. Check the calendar for upcoming events.

7 Steilacoom Tribal Cultural Center and Museum

1515 Lafayette St., Steilacoom, WA 98388; 253-584-6308
steilacoomtribe.business.site

Located in a church built in 1903, the museum celebrates Steilacoom culture and history

8 Suquamish Museum

6861 NE South St., Suquamish, WA 98392; 360-394-8499
suquamishmuseum.org

Sharing the lives, language, and culture of the Suquamish people, this museum curates exhibits and programs workshops and other events. While you're there, pay Chief Seattle's grave site a visit (it's just down the street).

9 Yakama Nation Museum & Cultural Center

100 Spiel-yi Loop, Toppenish, WA 98948; 509-865-2800
yakamamuseum.com

Home of the Yakama Nation Museum, Gift Shop, Heritage Theater, Library, and Winter Lodge, the Yakama Nation Cultural Center has been open since 1980. This makes it one of the oldest museums dedicated to sharing and preserving Indigenous peoples' culture and heritage. The museum has exhibits that showcase the history of the Yakama people, while the theater provides a community gathering space to watch films and performances. The center is open daily.

Also see Yakama Nation Treaty Day, page 93.

Indigenous Peoples' Museums

The Lewis and Clark Interpretive Center (see page 102) perches on a cliff overlooking the Pacific and the Columbia River.

WHAT DO YOU THINK OF when you think of Washington State history? The trips in this theme mostly revolve around the history of the state on its way to and since its statehood in 1889 (think homesteading, panning for gold, and excavating the Ozette Archaeological Site). In other themes, you'll find snippets of history dating back to the Missoula Floods. *See also Iron Goat Trail, page 112; Lady Washington, page 113; Glines Canyon Dam Removal Site, page 83; Dry Falls, page 9; Ephrata Fan, page 9; Twin Sisters Rock, page 13; and Indigenous Peoples' Museums, page 95.*

WASHINGTON STATE HISTORY

1 Bill Speidel's Underground Tour

614 First Ave., Seattle, WA 98104; 206-682-4646
undergroundtour.com

View the Emerald City from the underground. Touring Seattle's sub-
terranean storefronts and interconnected tunnels is a unique way to
view the city that built itself on top of . . . itself. Tours last 75 minutes,
and sometimes special or themed tours are available. You'll learn
quirky facts and see history through a very specific lens. Pioneer
Square was, to European American settlers, the original downtown
Seattle, and it's oddly preserved the way the townspeople decided to
rebuild after The Great Fire. Go see for yourself.

2 Capitol Building

416 Sid Snyder Ave. SW, Olympia, WA 98504; 360-902-8880
des.wa.gov/services/facilities-leasing/capitol-campus/tours

When then-governor Isaac Stevens helped take the Washington
Territory in 1853, Olympia was designated the provisional capital. A
two-story building was put up overlooking Capitol Lake, with meetings
taking place there beginning in 1854. It wasn't until 1889 that
Washington officially became a state, but the general capital location
(of Olympia) stuck. After some tumult around land and construction
costs, the new Capitol Building was opened in 1905.

Today there are free walking tours of the Legislative Building regularly throughout the week. You'll see many notable architectural and
decorative details in and around the Legislative Building, Capitol
Building, and Temple of Justice, including Tiffany lamps, a Tivoli
Fountain replica, and a 10,000-pound chandelier.

The Capitol Campus has hosted many protests and strikes and is
where Washington Supreme Court decisions are handed down. Visit
to tour a building, see the veterans memorials, or learn more about
Washington's statehood.

3 | Fort Nisqually Living History Museum

5519 Five Mile Drive, Tacoma, WA 98407; 253-404-3970
metroparkstacoma.org/place/fort-nisqually-living-history-museum

Known for its experiential learning and historic preservation, Fort Nisqually Living History Museum showcases collections of artifacts from European American homesteads and Indigenous people's textile arts, and features exhibits and gardens. Several events take place here throughout the year, including an escape room complete with a backstory based on the fort's history. Good luck.

4 | Hanford Nuclear Reservation (and B Reactor Tour)

2000 Logston Blvd., Richland, WA 99354; 509-376-1647
manhattanprojectbreactor.hanford.gov; b-reactor.org

This is the place to discover another notable and tragic part of Washington State history, to be sure. Part of the top-secret Manhattan Project, the B Reactor National Historic Landmark is the site of the plutonium reactor used to produce the atomic bomb that was dropped on Nagasaki, Japan, ending World War II and killing about 75,000 people. Tours here relay information about the scientific and engineering efforts that led to the creation of Fat Man, the effects of which have lasted for generations.

Located in the remote shrub-steppe desert of eastern Washington, Hanford feels simultaneously peaceful and postapocalyptic (the evacuation signs certainly contribute to the disaster vibe). Free tours are available through the U.S. Department of Energy; they're about 4 hours long and include a bus ride with interpretation, and a tour of the industrial-scale nuclear reactor. See also Hanford Reach National Monument, page 10.

5 | Japanese American Exclusion Memorial

4192 Eagle Harbor Drive, Bainbridge Island, WA 98110; 206-855-9038
bijac.org

Executive Order 9066. This was the order that forced Japanese and Japanese Americans into concentration camps from 1942 to 1945, during World War II. Bainbridge Island was home to many Japanese families who were forcibly relocated with only six days' notice. The Japanese American Exclusion Memorial commemorates them. The names of the 276 Japanese and Japanese American residents of Bainbridge Island are on the cedar wall. The Japanese phrase *Nidoto nai yoni,* or "let it not happen again," echoes from this place, which serves to honor and remember not only the Bainbridge Island residents who were relocated but also Japanese and Japanese Americans across the United States.

6 Lewis and Clark Interpretive Center

244 Robert Gray Drive, Ilwaco, WA 98624; 360-642-3029
parks.state.wa.us/187/cape-disappointment

Overlooking the water at Cape Disappointment State Park, the Lewis and Clark Interpretive Center tells the tale of the transcontinental journey of Meriwether Lewis and William Clark—how they made it to the Pacific Ocean. The Corps of Discovery Expedition, commissioned by Thomas Jefferson, lasted from 1804 to 1806. It was the first American expedition from the East Coast to cross the western part of the United States (the Louisiana Purchase had just been made in 1803).

The goal of the expedition was to map the territory, find a route west, and establish trade relationships with the Indigenous communities along the way (and to create an American foothold in the West before Great Britain and other European nations got there). European Americans had been to Washington before, but by boat (see *Lady Washington,* page 112). Lewis and Clark reported back with the commercial opportunities they observed, many maps, and other details from their journals (including a record of plants and animals found in the regions they traversed). Of the 33 people on the expedition, the most famous besides Lewis and Clark was their guide, Sacagawea, a Lemhi Shoshone woman who was, remarkably, caring for her infant son during the journey.

7 Logging and Mill Tour

1411 S. Forks Ave., Forks, WA 98331; 360-374-2531
forkswa.com/event/logging-mill-tour-2

The Forks Chamber of Commerce gives free logging and mill tours. Make a reservation, wear closed-toe shoes, and arrive 15 minutes ahead of schedule. On the tour you'll make several stops and admire several trees (those still standing and those being processed). You'll get an inside look at the modern-day logging industry and lumber mills. This might be especially exciting to gearheads, engineers, and those with an interest in the timber industry. The machinery and equipment are certainly a sight to see.

8 Makah Cultural and Research Center/ Cape Flattery

1880 Bayview Ave., Neah Bay, WA 98357; 360-645-2711
makahmuseum.com

Let's start with the basics. The Makah Cultural and Research Center is home to the Makah Museum, store, and language program—and it's where you purchase your recreation permits to hike on Makah land. But it is also the home of a collection of artifacts recovered from the Ozette Archaeological Site, which are interpreted by the Makah Museum. For those unfamiliar with this site, it is impressive, to say the least.

In 1970 a storm caused hundreds of wood artifacts to rise from the banks near the village of Ozette, which was a bit strange because wood normally decomposes pretty quickly. When the excavation began a few months later, what emerged was a near-perfectly preserved village that had been lost to a landslide around 500 years ago. Because of the way the landslide occurred, structures were left essentially intact underground. An 11-year excavation revealed six longhouses and their contents—some 50,000 artifacts spanning up to 2,000 years of Makah history. The site has been referred to as the Pompeii of America.

This was an incredibly important discovery. The history of the Makah people, their culture, and their way of life was preserved in artifacts—including knives, toys, and depictions of whale and seal hunting. This is especially powerful for defending traditional land, water, and hunting rights.

See also Makah Days, page 92.

9 Olmstead Place Historical State Park

921 Ferguson Road, Ellensburg, WA 98926; 509-925-1943
parks.state.wa.us/556/olmstead-place

Formerly a beef-turned-dairy farm worked by three generations of the pioneering Olmstead family beginning in 1875, this site was donated as a state park in 1968. It encompasses 221 acres just outside of Ellensburg. You can either hike the interpretive trail and wander at your leisure, or take a tour. There's an original log cabin with old furniture and homesteading artifacts inside, as well as barns, gardens, a creek, and machinery. If you want a peek into how some homesteaders set up their farms, this is a good spot for it.

10 Recreational Gold Panning

Statewide on land managed by the U.S. Forest Service and Bureau of
Land Management
dnr.wa.gov/publications/ger_gold_panning.pdf

Maybe if you grew up in Washington State, your family took you
panning for gold in your youth. I, on the other hand, just heard
about people flocking to the West Coast for the gold rush, which
hit Washington a bit later than California.

A panning tray costs only about $10–$20, and you can learn how
to pan by watching a YouTube video. To make this trip work, I recommend doing a bit of research in advance. There are several rivers
where the presence of gold has been reported, but not all of them
allow panning. Consult the Washington State Department of Natural
Resources (link above) to learn more about how to pan and where
you are and are not allowed to pan. Be patient, and good luck!

See also Klondike Gold Rush National Historical Park, page 47.

Panning for gold takes a lot of patience and a bit of luck.

The busiest locks in the United States are in the Ballard neighborhood of Seattle (see page 108).

WASHINGTON STATE, BIRTHPLACE OF BOEING, takes airplanes seriously. And ships and railroads have historically been important for fishing, trade, and the transport of goods and resources. Whether you're a history buff; a tinkerer; or a kid who dreams of becoming a pilot, a captain, or a conductor, there are many places to visit to feel inspired and learn.

RAILROADS, AIRPLANES, AND SHIPS

107

1 Ballard Locks

3015 NW 54th St., Seattle, WA 98107; 206-783-7059
ballardlocks.org

Ballard has the busiest locks in the United States. Free guided tours are offered throughout the year, or you can experience the locks at your own pace. First, wander around the beautiful Carl S. English Jr. Botanical Garden, and make your way to the visitor center and museum to learn more about the history of the Hiram M. Chittenden Locks, which were first opened in 1917. Then head outside to see the locks in action. You can walk over to watch as the water levels are adjusted and boats are let through from Lake Union to Puget Sound (and vice versa). Continue on to see steelhead trout and sockeye, Chinook, and coho salmon run through the locks (salmon are running June–September; if they aren't in, you can still admire the fish-ladder viewing room).

Consider scheduling a boat tour or renting a kayak if you'd like to pass through the locks as part of the boat traffic. If you're lucky enough to catch one of the locks closed for construction or maintenance, it's pretty cool to see them empty too!

2 Boeing Future of Flight Aviation Center

8415 Paine Field Blvd., Mukilteo, WA 98275; 800-464-1476
futureofflight.org

This is the only place in North America where you can tour a commercial jet assembly plant, according to the center's website. The tour, which involves a bit of walking, along with shuttle rides, takes place over an hour and a half. Arrive early, as the shuttle *will* leave without you. You'll be exploring the largest building in the world by volume (makes sense, as it has to assemble jets). If you visit on a weekday, there will be more people working down on the floor of the plant. Boeing 747, 767, 777, and 787 Dreamliner aircraft are all assembled here. You might catch some planes taking off and landing too! And, if you're like my brother-in-law, you will soon be able to identify exactly which model is flying overhead (if not, you can just ask Siri). There are also free exhibits and displays, and a store where you can pick up a souvenir on your way out.

3 The Center for Wooden Boats

1010 Valley St., Seattle, WA 98109; 206-382-2628
1880 SW Camano Drive, Camano Island, WA 98282; 360-387-9361
cwb.org

Part museum, part livery, part hands-on education, The Center for Wooden Boats brings maritime heritage to life for everyone in the community. It has a fleet of boats docked in South Lake Union (and at Cama Beach) as living museum pieces available to rent. It also has exhibits, lectures, and sailing and woodworking courses, and free public sails are held every Sunday year-round, rain or shine. The museum is free of charge, as are several other programs, such as tugboat story time.

If you are an experienced sailor, you'll need to do a check-out sail (about 30 minutes) to demonstrate your skills. Once you pass this test, you can rent sailboats. Membership and pass options are available, depending on how often you plan to be out on the water. You can also check out traditional rowboats and pedal boats, or you could charter a boat for a cruise around the lake. Keep your eye out for the Lake Union Wooden Boat Festival each year (lately, it's been in September).

4 Chehalis-Centralia Railroad & Museum

1101 SW Sylvenus St., Chehalis, WA 98532; 360-748-9593
steamtrainride.com

Take a ride on a 1916 steam train through the Chehalis River Valley. The restored coaches offer brunches, dinners, and other events, like mystery trains. This heritage railroad route is owned by the Port of Chehalis and is operated as a piece of Northwestern history. The ride is about 1.25–2 hours.

5 Fireboat *Duwamish*

Naval Reserve Armory, 860 Terry Ave. N., Seattle, WA 98109; 206-999-5107
fireboatduwamish.com

Fireboat *Duwamish* is a National Historic Landmark moored in South Lake Union, Seattle. You can go visit and board the boat at the Historic Ships Wharf. *Duwamish* is the second-oldest fireboat in the United States (it first launched in 1909). Since fighting its last fire in 1984, it has become a nonprofit organization whose mission includes preserving and restoring the boat, along with sharing its history as a maritime firefighting vessel. Go see this Seattle landmark for yourself—maybe bring your dog (dogs are welcome aboard) or your kids.

6 Hydroplane & Raceboat Museum

5917 S. 196th St., Kent, WA 98032; 206-764-9453
thunderboats.ning.com

The Hydroplane & Raceboat Museum is well known for its boat restorations. Some boats have been restored to working condition after racing some 50–90 years ago. The museum has loads of footage of races in its video vault, along with trophies, memorabilia, and stories of the greats.

The museum also hosts events and continues to share the legacy and history of hydroplane boat racing. It provides programming to engage youth in STEM education (Victory Education Program), summer camps, and J-Hydro Racing. The junior racing program provides space for families to work together to build a boat for their child (ages 9–16) to race. It's a unique opportunity for families to work together to build something—and for kids to race a pretty fast boat on the water.

7 Iron Goat Trail

GPS Coordinates (Martin Creek): N47° 43.578' W121° 12.077' (Forest Service Road 6710, Leavenworth, WA 98826); 360-677-2414
GPS Coordinates (Iron Goat): N47° 42.681' W121° 09.716' (Old Cascade Highway, Leavenworth, WA 98826)
GPS Coordinates (Wellington): N47° 44.835' W121° 07.625' (Tye Scenic Road, Leavenworth, WA 98826)
irongoattrail.org; fs.usda.gov/recarea/mbs/recreation/recarea/?recid=17892

You can access Iron Goat Trail from the Martin Creek, Wellington, or Iron Goat trailhead. If you start at Martin Creek, you'll enjoy a mostly flat 6-mile round-trip hike along the old railroad grade. There will be interpretive signage along the way. The abandoned town of Wellington sits at the other end of the trail. This is why you're here.

The 1910 Wellington Avalanche was responsible for one of America's worst railroad disasters of all time. It had been snowing for days. Trains patiently waited out the storm at the station because the tracks were too snowy to clear. Passengers and railway employees slept on board. Then, after midnight on March 1, it happened: The avalanche swept the trains from the tracks, knocked them nearly down the mountainside, and buried them in snow. Only 23 people survived; 96 were killed.

Within a few years, Wellington was renamed Tye, and snowsheds were built above the tracks to protect against future avalanches. You can see those today as you're hiking in the area. These tracks aren't used anymore since a new tunnel was built in 1929 at a lower elevation. Do not enter any of the old tunnels; they're unsafe. If you hike along the upper trail section of Iron Goat Trail, you can see the railroad tracks still in use today.

Iron Goat Trail

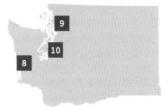

8 Lady Washington

500 N. Custer St., Aberdeen, WA 98520; 800-200-5239
historicalseaport.org/ships/lady-washington; historicalseaport.org/tickets

The original *Lady Washington* sailed during the Revolutionary War before voyaging from Boston around Cape Horn to the northwest coast of North America—the first American ship to do so. After successful sails to conduct trade (or try to) in Hong Kong (China), Japan, and Honolulu, it eventually wrecked in 1797 in the Philippines.

Grays Harbor Historical Seaport brought together historians and shipwrights in Aberdeen to construct a modern, full-scale replica of the brig using traditional methods and materials for Washington State's centennial. Its first launch was in 1989. Two of my siblings-in-law have worked as sailors on *Lady Washington,* so there were a few years when I'd pay attention to where she was docked each day in case I could catch them for a visit in Bellingham or Port Townsend. You can find both *Lady Washington* and *Hawaiian Chieftain* sailing up and down the West Coast each summer from California to British Columbia. There are many ports in Washington where she might dock to welcome passengers aboard for tours, sails, educational programming, and special events (like pirate and battle sails, which I think the ship perfected when it starred in *Pirates of the Caribbean: The Curse of the Black Pearl).*

Lady Washington is also Washington's state ship (see page 152).

9 Lake Whatcom Railway

5159 N. P. Road, Sedro-Woolley, WA 98284; 360-441-0719
lakewhatcomrailway.com

Up for a ride? This authentic steam locomotive takes you on a trip down the Northern Pacific Railroad, leaving from Wickersham. The passenger coaches serve as a way to experience our country's railway heritage firsthand and learn from knowledgeable volunteers about the cars' history. The train cars have been in continuous operation since the early 1900s. There aren't many amenities on board (just a small coffee shop train car). Keep your eye out for a number of special event rides throughout the year (Father's Day ride, pumpkin patch ride, and so on). If you love old trains, this trip is for you. Expect a charming ride and scenery along the way.

⑩ Museum of Flight

9404 E. Marginal Way S., Seattle, WA 98108; 206-764-5700
museumofflight.org

This air and space museum wows. You can see biplanes, helicopters, and spacecraft; you can go on an interactive tour, a virtual-reality trip to the moon, or a pilot experience; or you can complete a space mission at the Challenger Learning Center. There are flight simulators, movies in the 3-D theater, STEM learning programs, and hands-on workshops for the whole family each weekend. With so much to offer, the Museum of Flight provides several options to customize your experience at different levels of admission. It can be a bit overwhelming, but the website has an option to plan your visit that narrows down your search based on some criteria about yourself. Or you can reach out to a coordinator at the museum for help. Whatever you decide to do, you're bound to learn a lot—and have a ton of fun.

The *Lady Washington* (see opposite and page 152) is a replica of the ship of the same name that landed on the West Coast from Boston in the 1700s.

11 12

11 Museum of History & Industry

860 Terry Ave. N., Seattle, WA 98109; 206-324-1126
mohai.org

The Museum of History & Industry walks visitors through the journey of industry in Washington State, from when the European American settlers arrived in the Northwest, meeting local Indigenous communities, to the building of an industrial hub—from timber and trains to tech. The Bezos Center for Innovation addition, opened in 2013, created an exhibit to speak to innovation at large, and in Seattle specifically. *True Northwest* and *Maritime Seattle* are other favorite exhibits. Check what will be featured on the dates you'll be in town!

Seattle's Museum of History & Industry (MOHAI), on Lake Union

The train depot in Snoqualmie—ride the train from here to the Northwest Railway Museum!

12 Northwest Railway Museum

38625 SE King St., Snoqualmie, WA 98065; 425-888-3030
trainmuseum.org

If you're looking for a train that's more than a train, this one's for you. This museum and railway offer weekend rides and special events. For little ones (or superfans), there's an annual event called Day Out with Thomas, where Thomas the Tank Engine pulls your train. You can arrive to the Railway History Center by car or train and see the trains on exhibit. Learn about how trains and railroads in general changed the Northwest. If you're interested in seeing a train being worked on (no guarantees), they take appointments at the Conservation and Restoration Center.

If what you're after is the historical train depot, it's open daily, 10 a.m.–5 p.m., except New Year's Day, Thanksgiving Day, and Christmas Day. It has been restored to its 1890 condition. If you're planning to take the train to the museum, you can buy your ticket at the original window.

13 Washington State Ferries

Statewide
wsdot.com/ferries

You don't need to take a special tour or sail your own boat to enjoy being on the water in Washington State. Pick a place to go and take a ferry there. You can go to San Juan Island, Kingston, Bremerton, or Vashon. You can drive, bike, or walk on. The perfect Seattle morning? Leave downtown Seattle on a ferry to Bainbridge Island, grab a coffee on Bainbridge (there are cafés within walking distance of the ferry terminal), and ferry back. Those Seattle skyline views! Whether it's sunny, rainy, or foggy, they're always awesome. I've been to at least 14 ferry terminals in Washington, and I have never been disappointed by a ferry commute, once I make it on the ferry. (You can reserve in advance on many routes). The wind—my gosh, the wind!—the sunshine, the fog, the land in the distance, the little mountainous islands you pass by . . . I could go on. I love this state, especially from the water.

A Washington State Ferry with the Olympic Mountains in the distance

Paradise Inn, Mount Rainier National Park (see page 123)

ADMIRERS OF DESIGN AND HISTORY, take note. There are some beautiful and interesting buildings in Washington State—some by renowned architects, and others (no less impressive) designed by the lesser-known. Some are part of campuses, others are public buildings like the Renton Library, and others are private but take appointments. Gaze on, photograph, explore, and tour these very cool structures.

HISTORICAL BUILDINGS AND ARCHITECTURE

(continued on next page)

Located on Marrowstone Island, Fort Flagler (see page 122) was once an active U.S. Army installation.

Fort Flagler

10541 Flagler Road, Nordland, WA 98358; 360-385-3701
parks.state.wa.us/364/fort-flagler

Built in the 1890s and located at the northernmost tip of Marrowstone Island, Fort Flagler is part of the Triangle of Fire (along with Fort Casey and Fort Worden). These three forts are situated in a triangle at the entrance to Puget Sound from the Strait of Juan de Fuca. Once an active U.S. Army fort (1899–1953), Fort Flagler is now a museum, gift shop, and state park. There are a number of bunkers and batteries you can explore on your own or on a tour. The park is a strange mix of natural beauty, retired structures, and wartime equipment. Old officers' quarters and other buildings can be rented out as vacation homes. And the grounds have plenty of space for you to camp, hike, kayak, or dig for clams. If you want to make the trip a twofer, Fort Worden is just across the water in Port Townsend and has a ton of cool fort ruins to explore as well. See Fort Worden State Park, page 34. (Fort Casey is across the water in the other direction; see Admiralty Head Lighthouse, page 24).

Gas Works Park

2101 N. Northlake Way, Seattle, WA 98103; 206-684-4075
seattle.gov/parks/find/parks/gas-works-park

Once a plant that converted coal to natural gas in a process called gasification, Seattle Gas Light Company began a new life in 1975, when it opened as a public park spanning 20 acres, complete with a play area, reservable pavilions, and rolling grass hills with views of Seattle's skyline. The ruins of the rusty gasworks make for strange and wonderful backdrops for picnics, photography shoots, and LARP (live-action role-playing). You may also remember it as the set for an epic paintball battle between Kat and Patrick in *10 Things I Hate About You,* a classic film from 1999. If you'd rather be on the water with a view of the park, there are places along Lake Union that rent kayaks, paddleboards, and even pedal boats (yes, like the one Kat and Patrick used).

3 Maryhill Museum and Stonehenge

35 Maryhill Museum of Art Drive, Goldendale, WA 98620; Stonehenge Drive, Maryhill, WA 98620; 509-773-3733
maryhillmuseum.org; maryhillmuseum.org/outside/stonehenge-memorial

Sam Hill was a rich Quaker man who had ventures in railroads, highways, and utilities. He invested in the stock market, and in some wild ideas. Hill erected the first World War I memorial in the form of a to-scale replica of Stonehenge, dedicated to the men of Klickitat who died serving. The reinforced concrete structure stands on the bluff above the Columbia River Gorge in southwest Washington—in the right light, the view is heart-stopping. It's no wonder Hill wanted this site for his Utopian Quaker village. Unfortunately, no one joined him to turn the community into a reality. The mansion he began building eventually became the Maryhill Museum (3 miles west of his Stonehenge). The museum and its grounds have permanent and rotating collections, and you can learn more about Sam Hill's life and legend.

4 MoPOP

325 Fifth Ave. N., Seattle, WA 98109; 206-770-2700
mopop.org/about-mopop/mission/architecture-of-the-mopop-building

First opened as EMP (Experience Music Project) in 2000, the Museum of Popular Culture, or MoPOP, is a love letter to popular culture. There are permanent and special/traveling exhibitions on several aspects of pop culture, including music, film, television, and video games.

Whether or not you go inside the museum, circumnavigate it. The design, architect Frank Gehry said, was inspired by deconstructed guitars from which he created early models. The rock-and-roll feel translates through the shape, which resembles a visual representation of sound waves. The colors are also fluid—different panels have different finishes that shift and change in the light. It's hard not to notice MoPOP when it first comes into view. And once you notice it, it's hard not to keep noticing it, watching its waves from different angles— a beautiful signifier of the ever-evolving nature of popular culture. Interior building tours are free with admission to the museum.

5 Paradise Inn, Mount Rainier National Park

52807 Paradise Road E., Ashford, WA 98304; 360-569-2275
nps.gov/articles/paradise-inn-a-history-of-beauty-and-challenge.htm;
mtrainierguestservices.com/about-us/history/history-paradise-inn

Open mid-May–early October, Paradise Inn has a grand, rustic American vibe (that's a thing). With a steep pitched roof, a behemoth exposed-timber frame, twin fireplaces, and stonework, Paradise Inn is a beauty

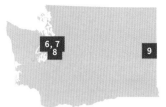

of a National Historic Landmark. Mount Rainier was established as the United States' fifth national park in 1899. By 1917 Paradise Inn had opened its doors at 5,420 feet elevation. According to the National Park Service website, Mount Rainier has the largest glacier system in the Lower 48, thanks to Paradise's average annual snowfall of 640 inches (53.3 feet). That's a lot of snow—it's no wonder the inn and annex have needed restoration throughout the years. With the warmer weather, wildflowers bloom. While the inn has updated plumbing and electricity—and meets seismic codes—it doesn't fuss with modern frills like televisions or Wi-Fi. Have a seat by the fire—Paradise feels like paradise.

6 Pioneer Square

Pioneer Building, 600 First Ave., Seattle, WA 98104; 206-667-0687
pioneersquare.org

This groovy, old part of the city has a checkered history. When European American settlers arrived on the scene, Duwamish and Suquamish people had been living in the area for thousands of years. They lived in several villages across what we know today as Pioneer Square. The area quickly became the European Americans' preferred downtown location. The Treaty of Point Elliott was signed in 1855; the Battle of Seattle was in 1856. The European Americans continued building and worked to keep Native Americans out of Pioneer Square (the city council issued an order to ban Indigenous people from the city of Seattle, their ancestral lands). Later, in 1882, the Chinese Exclusion Act was signed. Seattle's white workers had a growing anti-Chinese sentiment that led to a riot in 1886 and spurred many Chinese Americans (who were denied naturalization rights and property rights) to move to San Francisco.

After Seattle's Great Fire of 1889, nearly everything needed to be rebuilt. Chinese Americans contributed to much of the labor force. Most of the old brick buildings you see in Pioneer Square today were built in the decade following the fire. Take a walking tour around the neighborhood. New posh restaurants and cocktail bars will often have a plaque on their façade acknowledging their history. While you can truly stroll anywhere in Pioneer Square and look up at the old brick buildings, if you need a little guidance, start with the Pioneer Building (1892), Merchant's Cafe (1890), The J&M Cafe (1889), and the Moses Building (1900). Each has a story to tell.

7 Rainier Tower

1301 Fifth Ave., Seattle, WA 98101
rainiersquare.com

Rainier Tower looks ordinary enough from its 12th story up; it's when your eye hits the 11-story concrete base of the building that you might tilt your head. The bottom tapers in so that the entire building is standing on a pedestal half the width of the building above. Completed in 1977, it is sometimes referred to as the Beaver Building because it appears as though a giant beaver has chomped the base in an effort to fell the tower. Despite its somewhat precarious appearance, Rainier Tower has been deemed earthquake resistant. Architect Minoru Yamasaki designed the footprint to maintain as much space as possible for an outdoor square. Rainier Square is being revamped with the new and shiny addition of Rainier Square Tower right next door—it has its own shape, at once a complement to the old and something altogether new.

8 Renton Public Library

100 Mill Ave. S., Renton, WA 98057; 425-226-6043
kcls.org/locations/1556

This Renton Public Library branch is literally a bridge from downtown to Liberty Park. Views from the library of the Cedar River below have been admired since it opened in 1966. It recently underwent renovations to meet today's energy and seismic standards. If your timing is right, you can watch coho, Chinook, and sockeye salmon run up the Cedar to their spawning grounds. Otherwise, have a seat and read a book—or daydream and stare out the floor-to-ceiling windows.

9 Riverfront Park, United States Pavilion

507 N. Howard St., Spokane, WA 99201; 509-625-6600
my.spokanecity.org/riverfrontspokane

Even before Expo '74 came to town, Spokane knew the world's fair was a great opportunity to reinvent the downtown area and bring Spokane Falls back into the spotlight. For decades, train tracks, trestles, and warehouses had been about all you could see near the river. This was the first environmentally themed World's Fair, and hosted by the smallest city, putting Spokane on the map in more ways than one.

After the Expo, Spokane got a 100-acre park, Riverfront Park. The park and the United States Pavilion from 1974 were renovated and reopened in 2019. The pavilion is now a multifunctional event venue with an elevated stage. Shading elements have been added to provide respite on hot, sunny days, and LED lighting has been installed in the arching net of the pavilion. The illumination blades incorporated in the design can provide subtle, functional lighting or create dramatic displays of different colors. The park now has an elevated skybridge near the pavilion that provides 360-degree views of Spokane, and developments are still underway. An interactive playground is set to open in 2020. There will be slides, water features, and a skate park. The United States Pavilion, a historic landmark, looks better than ever. And the Spokane River continues, rightly so, to be the focus of Riverfront Park.

10 Seattle Public Library– Central Library Branch

1000 Fourth Ave., Seattle, WA 98104; 206-386-4636
spl.org/hours-and-locations/central-library

Formal reading rooms and libraries began popping up in Seattle in the early 1890s. After several moves—and a fire that took 25,000 books with it—a new library was opened in 1906 between Fourth and Fifth Avenues between Madison and Spring Streets, where the Seattle Central Library stands today. Though the location has remained the same, the building was replaced in 1960 (complete with a drive-through book-return window), and again in 2004 (with a book-return conveyor belt).

It its newest incarnation, the library is mostly glass and steel with interesting shapes, free public computers, fun colors, reading rooms, music practice rooms, an auditorium, and mixed-use spaces. My favorite part (besides the floor that is entirely red—13 shades in all directions) might be the uninterrupted Books Spiral. You don't even realize how many floors you've traversed because you are occupied eyeing the shelves and shelves of tomes as you walk up the gradually sloping floors. Just me?

The library is 11 stories and full of function and whimsy. A reading room on the 10th floor provides pretty rad views. Architects Rem

Koolhaas and Joshua Prince-Ramus let form follow function and designed a space to accommodate growth, the importance of digital media alongside print, and a social gathering space (where you don't have to talk to anyone if you don't want to). Personally, I can spend hours here. If you have a group of five or more, you can request a free architecture tour of the building (in advance), or you can take a self-guided tour.

11 Smith Tower

506 Second Ave., Seattle, WA 98104; 206-624-0414
smithtower.com

Smith Tower is the oldest skyscraper in Seattle. When it was built, in 1914, its 38 stories made it the tallest building west of the Mississippi. Perched in historic Pioneer Square, Smith Tower offers 360-degree views from its open-air observation deck. If you have a group of 6–20, you can book a 1-hour guided tour. Otherwise, consider a ticket to the observatory, which includes a trip up to the 35th floor in the original Otis elevators. There's a speakeasy-esque bar and food options available as well.

12 Space Needle and Seattle Center Monorail

Space Needle: 400 Broad St., Seattle, WA 98109; 206-905-2100
Seattle Center Monorail has stations at Westlake Center and Seattle Center;
206-905-2620
spaceneedle.com; seattlemonorail.com

Making its debut at the 1962 World's Fair, the Space Needle was meant to come down afterward. Instead, it has become an icon of Seattle. Recent renovations have brought the building's wow factor up several notches. The needle now contains the world's only rotating glass floor, an open-air observation deck with floor-to-sky glass walls, and multi-level floor-to-ceiling windows inside. There used to be several feet of wall before the windows started, but now there is glass and more glass. With 360-degree indoor and outdoor views of Seattle and beyond (Mount Rainier, Mount Baker, the Cascades, the Olympics, and Puget Sound), the Space Needle is an experience not to miss.

To double your world's fair factor, ride the monorail to or from the Space Needle. Ticket prices are comparable to a ride on public transit. Your ride will provide a unique elevated view as you travel down Fifth Avenue. According to its website, Seattle's monorail was the first full-scale commercial monorail in the country. Trains depart every 10 minutes.

13 Spokane County Courthouse

1116 W. Broadway Ave., Spokane, WA 99260; 509-477-5790
spokanecounty.org/3958/Courthouse-Tours

A beautiful building on the north bank of the Spokane River, the Spokane County Courthouse has been said to resemble a castle straight out of France. The architect, W. A. Ritchie, was selected during a design competition for the new courthouse in 1893; two years later the court's doors opened. The turrets, the tower, the curved lines, and the slate-shingled roof are all marvels in their own right. While there aren't any guided tours, the public is welcome to tour the building (or sit in on court proceedings, unless otherwise posted).

14 Stadium High School

111 NE St., Tacoma, WA 98403
prettygrittytours.com/stadium-high-tour.html

I went to public high school, and my high school did not look like this. Stadium High School is a brick castle—complete with turrets and ocean views. In fact, my friend's office was in one of the turrets. What luck! Originally the building was meant to be a hotel—the grandest hotel, with French architectural inspiration and accommodations so posh all other hotels would cower in embarrassment. The Panic of 1893, an economic depression, sent many communities spinning. Demolition of the would-be hotel was underway when some kind souls thought to repurpose it as a high school. In 1906 the school was opened. By 1910 the adjoining stadium had been built, leading the school to update its name from Tacoma High School to Stadium High School in 1913. This day trip also happens to be another nod to *10 Things I Hate About You*—the stadium is the one in which a Mr. Patrick Verona (played by Heath Ledger) sang a ditty to Ms. Kat Stratford (Julia Stiles). Kat Stratford deserved better.

Because this is still a high school, you can't just walk in (but you can walk by!). Late-night tours are offered; book at the website above.

The Suzzallo Library at the University of Washington is a stunning Gothic structure.

15 Suzzallo Library

4000 15th Ave. NE, Seattle, WA 98195; 206-543-0242
lib.washington.edu/suzzallo

This ornate collegiate Gothic library, named for University of Washington's late president Henry Suzzallo, is made up of four buildings built over a period of 60-plus years. In 1926 the Suzzallo Library's main library building opened. The original three-part plan was revised to accommodate a new aesthetic and a fourth structure. Several buildings on the University of Washington's campus are beautiful, but the library is especially grand. Its reading room rivals any you can think of—it's 250 feet long, with bright lacquered wood and 65-foot-high ceilings. There are details everywhere—from representations of Washington State's plant life adorning the bookcases to sculpted terra-cotta figures in niches on the exterior. Virtual and in-person tours are available.

Leavenworth hosts many festivals throughout the year. And yes, there's an Oktoberfest.

FESTIVALS ARE CELEBRATIONS, and Washington has a wide variety of things to celebrate. There are festivals to celebrate a crop, a season, or an art form. There are cultural, agricultural, heritage, music, film, art, theater, and sports festivals. There are fairs and markets and religious festivals. There is pride, there is patriotism, and there are tulips.

FESTIVALS

Food/Agricultural

Ballard SeafoodFest
5345 Ballard Ave. NW, Seattle, WA 98107
seafoodfest.org

Bite of Seattle
Seattle Center, 305 Harrison St., Seattle, WA 98109; 425-295-3262
biteofseattle.com

Issaquah Salmon Days
Front Street North, Issaquah, WA 98027
issaquahchamber.com/salmondays

Lavender Festival
Carrie Blake Community Park, 202 N. Blake Ave., Sequim, WA 98382; 360-681-3035
lavenderfestival.com

Leavenworth Oktoberfest
Front Street between 10th and 12th Streets, Leavenworth, WA 98826; 209-264-1852
leavenworthoktoberfest.com

National Lentil Festival
Spring Street and Reaney Park, Pullman, WA 99163; 800-365-6948
lentilfest.com

Northwest Raspberry Festival
518 Front St., Lynden, WA 98264; 360-354-5995
facebook.com/Northwest-Raspberry-Festival-328339560562995

OysterFest
250 W. Sanderson Way, Shelton, WA 98584
oysterfest.org

Pig Out in the Park
Riverfront Park, North Howard Street, Spokane, WA 99201; 509-921-5579
spokanepigout.com

(continued on next page)

Tulip Festival
311 W. Kincaid St., Mount Vernon, WA 98273; 360-428-5959
tulipfestival.org

Vashon Island Strawberry Festival
11726 Vashon Highway SW, Vashon, WA 98070; 206-463-6217
vashonchamber.com/strawberryfestival

Washington State Apple Blossom Festival
Wenatchee Convention Center, 121 N. Wenatchee Ave., Wenatchee, WA 98801;
509-662-3616
appleblossom.org

Music

Bumbershoot
Seattle Center, 305 Harrison St., Seattle, WA 98109
bumbershoot.com

Capitol Hill Block Party
1122 E. Pike St., Seattle, WA 98122
capitolhillblockparty.com

Doe Bay Fest
Doe Bay Resort & Retreat, 107 Doe Bay Road, Olga, WA 98279; 360-376-2291
doebay.com/doe-bay-fest-2

Hempfest
Myrtle Edwards Park, 3130 Alaskan Way, Seattle, WA 98121; 206-364-4367
hempfest.org

Northwest Folklife
Seattle Center, 305 Harrison St., Seattle, WA 98109; 206-684-7300
nwfolklife.org

Olympia Music Festival
Fort Worden State Park, 200 Battery Way, Port Townsend, WA 98368; 360-385-9699
olympicmusicfestival.org

THING Festival
Fort Worden, 200 Battery Way, Port Townsend, WA 98368; 206-467-5510
thingnw.org

Volume Inlander Music Festival
Multiple venues in downtown Spokane
volume.inlander.com

Watershed
Gorge Amphitheatre, 754 Silica Road NW, George, WA 98848
watershedfest.com

Film

Local Sightings
Northwest Film Forum, 1515 12th Ave., Seattle, WA 98122; 206-329-2629
nwfilmforum.org/festivals/local-sightings-film-festival-pacific-nw

SIFF
305 Harrison St., Seattle, WA 98109; 206-464-5830
siff.net

Translations
1620 12th Ave., Seattle, WA 98122; 206-323-4274
threedollarbillcinema.org/programs/translations

Seattle Queer Film Festival
1620 12th Ave., Seattle, WA 98122
threedollarbillcinema.org/seaqueerfilmfest

Cultural

Argosy Christmas Ship Festival
1101 Alaskan Way, Pier 55, Seattle, WA 98101, and other locations; 888-623-1445
argosycruises.com/argosy-cruises/christmas-ship-festival

Buckley Log Show
375 N. River Ave., Buckley, WA 98321
cityofbuckley.com/logshow

Chinatown-International District Dragon Fest
South King Street from Fifth Avenue to Maynard Avenue, Seattle, WA 98104; 206-382-1197
cidbia.org/events/dragonfest

Diwali: Lights of India
Armory Main Floor, Seattle Center, 305 Harrison St., Seattle, WA 98109
seattlecenter.com/events/event-calendar/diwali-lights-of-india

Festival Sundiata-Black Arts Fest
Seattle Center, 305 Harrison St., Seattle, WA 98109; 866-505-6006
festivalsundiata.org

Lunar New Year
Chinatown-International District, Seattle, WA 98104; 206-382-1197
cidbia.org/events/lunar-new-year

Pacific Northwest Scottish Highland Games
Enumclaw Expo Center, 45224 284th Ave. SE, Enumclaw, WA 98022; 206-522-2541
sshga.org

Pride (LGBTQ)
Bellingham: bellinghampride.org
Kitsap: kitsappride.org, 877-PRIDE-69 (774-3369)
Olympia: capitalcitypride.net
Seattle: seattlepride.org, 206-322-9561
Spokane: outspokane.org/pride-parade, 509-879-2820
Tacoma: tacomapride.org, 253-383-2318

(continued on next page)

Vashon Sheepdog Classic
Misty Isle Farms, 12011 SW 220th St., Vashon, WA 98070
vashonsheepdogclassic.com

Winter

Bavarian Icefest
Downtown Leavenworth, WA 98826; 509-548-5807
leavenworth.org

First Night Tacoma
Broadway between South Seventh and South 11th Streets, Tacoma, WA 98402;
253-591-5894
firstnighttacoma.org

Lake Chelan Winterfest
Downtown Chelan, WA 98816; 509-682-3503
lakechelan.com/winterfest

Timbrrr! Winter Music Festival
Leavenworth Festhalle, 1001 Front St., Leavenworth, WA 98826
winter.timbermusicfest.com

Miscellaneous

Ellensburg Rodeo
Ellensburg Rodeo Grounds, 1010 E. Eighth St., Ellensburg, WA 98926; 800-637-2444
ellensburgrodeo.com

Hoopfest
Downtown Spokane, WA 99201; 509-624-2414
spokanehoopfest.net

Seafair
Multiple locations including Genesee Park, 4316 S. Genesee St., Seattle, WA 98118;
206-728-0123
seafair.com

Walla Walla Balloon Stampede
Howard Tietan Park, 616 E. Tietan St., Walla Walla, WA 99362; 208-375-0512
wallawallaballoonstampede.com

Washington State Fair
Washington State Fair Events Center, 110 Ninth Ave. SW, Puyallup, WA 98371;
253-845-1771
thefair.com

Washington State International Kite Festival
World Kite Museum, 303 SW Sid Snyder Drive, Long Beach, WA 98631; 360-642-4020
kitefestival.com

Long Beach hosts the Washington State International Kite Festival during the third full week of August.

Root, root, root for the home team!

YOU CAN ALMOST ALWAYS FIND a game, match, bout, or meet to attend in Washington State. It has a plethora of college, pro, minor, and amateur leagues and teams to root for. Fellow fans are waiting for you to show up spirited to cheer on your favorite (or new-to-you) roller derby, rugby, basketball, soccer, hockey, football, and baseball teams. Fun fact: Seahawks fans have—more than once—held the record for loudest crowd at an outdoor stadium. You can't say I didn't warn you.

SPORTS

Baseball

Everett Aquasox (Class A Minor League Baseball [MiLB])
Everett Memorial Stadium, 3900 Broadway, Everett, WA 98201; 425-258-3673
milb.com/everett

Seattle Mariners (Major League Baseball)
T-Mobile Park, 1250 First Ave. S., Seattle, WA 98134; 206-346-4001
mlb.com/mariners

Spokane Indians (Class A MiLB)
Avista Stadium, 602 N. Havana St., Spokane, WA 99202; 509-343-6886
milb.com/spokane

Tacoma Rainiers (Triple-A MiLB)
Cheney Stadium, 2502 S. Tyler St., Tacoma, WA 98405; 253-752-7707
milb.com/tacoma

Tri-City Dust Devils (Class A MiLB)
Gesa Stadium, 6200 Burden Blvd., Pasco, WA 99301; 509-544-8789
milb.com/tri-city-dust-devils

Wenatchee Applesox (Collegiate Summer Baseball)
Paul Thomas Sr. Field, 1300 Fifth St., Wenatchee, WA 98801; 509-665-6900
applesox.com

Basketball

Seattle Storm (Women's National Basketball Association)
305 Harrison St., Seattle, WA 98109; 206-217-9622
Note: While part of their home arena is under construction, the Seattle Storm will play the 2021–22 season at Angel of the Winds Arena in Everett and at the University of Washington's Alaska Airlines Arena. (Seattle's Key Arena is scheduled to reopen in late 2021.)
storm.wnba.com

(continued on next page)

Football

Seattle Seahawks (National Football League)
CenturyLink Field, 800 Occidental Ave. S., Seattle, WA 98134; 888-635-4295
seahawks.com

Hockey

Everett Silvertips (Western Hockey League [WHL])
Angel of the Winds Arena, 2000 Hewitt Ave., Everett, WA 98201; 425-252-5100
everettsilvertips.com

Seattle Kraken (National Hockey League)
305 Harrison St., Seattle, WA 98109; 844-645-7825
nhl.com/kraken

Seattle Thunderbirds (WHL)
Accesso ShoWare Center, 625 W. James St., Kent, WA 98032; 253-239-7825
seattlethunderbirds.com

Spokane Chiefs (WHL)
Spokane Arena, 720 W. Mallon Ave., Spokane, WA 99201; 509-535-7825
spokanechiefs.com

Tri-City Americans (WHL)
Toyota Center, 7000 W. Grandridge Blvd., Kennewick, WA 99336; 509-736-0606
amshockey.com

Roller Derby

Bellingham Roller Betties
(Women's Flat Track Derby Association [WFTDA])
Whatcom Community College, 237 W. Kellogg Road, Bellingham, WA 98226
bellinghamrollerbetties.com

Dockyard Derby Dames (WFTDA)
Pierce College, 9401 Farwest Drive SW, Tacoma, WA 98498
dockyardderbydames.com

Jet City Roller Derby League (WFTDA)
Seaview Gym, Edmonds Community College, 20000 68th Ave. W., Lynnwood, WA 9803
jetcityrollerderby.com

Lilac City Roller Derby League (WFTDA)
Various Spokane-area locations, including Pattison's North, HUB Sports Center,
and Skate Line Inc.
lilaccityrollerderby.com

Oly Rollers (WFTDA)
Skateland Skate Center, 2725 12th Ave. NE, Olympia, WA 98506
facebook.com/olyrollers

Port Scandalous Roller Derby (WFTDA)
Boys & Girls Club, 400 W. Fir St., Sequim, WA 98382
facebook.com/portscandalousrollerderby

Puget Sound Outcast Derby (Men's Roller Derby Association)
Skate Deck Everett, 9700 19th Ave. SE, Everett, WA 98208
outcastderby.org

Rainy City Roller Dolls (WFTDA)
The Rollerdrome, 216 W. Maple St., Centralia, WA 98531
rainycityrollerdolls.com

Rat City Roller Derby League (WFTDA)
Various Seattle-area locations, including KeyArena and the Accesso ShoWare Center
ratcityrollerderby.com

Tilted Thunder Rail Birds (Roller Derby Coalition of Leagues)
Skate Deck Everett, 9700 19th Ave. SE, Everett, WA 98208
facebook.com/tiltedthunderrailbirds

Rugby

Seattle Seawolves (Major League Rugby)
Safire Sports, 14800 Starfire Way, Tukwila, WA 98188; 206-431-3232
seattleseawolves.com

Soccer

Reign FC (National Women's Soccer League)
Cheney Stadium, 2502 S. Tyler St., Tacoma, WA 98405
reignfc.com

Seattle Sounders FC (Major League Soccer)
CenturyLink Field, 800 Occidental Ave. S., Seattle, WA 98134; 877-MLS-GOAL
(657-4625)
soundersfc.com

Collegiate

Central Washington University Wildcats (NCAA* Division II)
Ellensburg, WA
wildcatsports.com

Eastern Washington University Eagles (NCAA Division I)
Cheney, WA
goeags.com

Evergreen State College Geoducks (NAIA**)
Olympia, WA
gogeoducks.com

(continued on next page)

*National Collegiate Athletic Association **National Association of Intercollegiate Athletics

Sports

Gonzaga University Bulldogs (NCAA Division I)
Spokane, WA
gozags.com

Pacific Lutheran University Lutes (NCAA Division III)
Tacoma, WA
golutes.com

Seattle University Redhawks (NCAA Division I)
Seattle, WA
goseattleu.com

University of Washington Huskies (NCAA Division I)
Seattle, WA
gohuskies.com

Washington State University Cougars (NCAA Division I)
Pullman, WA
wsucougars.com

Western Washington University Vikings (NCAA Division II)
Bellingham, WA
wwuvikings.com

Whitman College Blues (NCAA Division III)
Walla Walla, WA
athletics.whitman.edu

Whitworth University Pirates (NCAA Division III)
Spokane, WA
whitworthpirates.com

From lacrosse to professional football, Washington has a sport for you.

A snowboarder at Stevens Pass

WHEN THE MOUNTAINS GET SNOW, the people are happy. Skiers and snowshoers have several options for snow sports in the state. There are also groomed locations for snow sledding and tubing.

ENJOYING THE SNOW

Crystal Mountain
33914 Crystal Mountain Blvd., Enumclaw, WA 98022; 360-663-3050
www.crystalmountainresort.com

Gold Creek Sno-Park
Forest Service Road 4832, Snoqualmie Pass, WA 98068; 509-852-1100
tinyurl.com/goldcreeksno

Hyak Sno-Park
Snoqualmie Pass, WA 98068; 509-656-2230
snowrec.org/hyak

Mt. Baker Ski Area
Mount Baker Highway, Deming, WA 98244; 360-734-6771
mtbaker.us

Mt. Spokane
Part of Mount Spokane State Park, Mead, WA 99021; 509-238-4258
mtspokane.com

Stevens Pass
US 2, Skykomish, WA 98288; 206-812-4510
stevenspass.com

Suncadia
3600 Suncadia Trail, Cle Elum, WA 98922; 866-904-6300
destinationhotels.com/suncadia-resort/activities/winter-recreation

The Summit at Snoqualmie
1001 WA 906, Snoqualmie Pass, WA 98068; 425-434-7669
summitatsnoqualmie.com

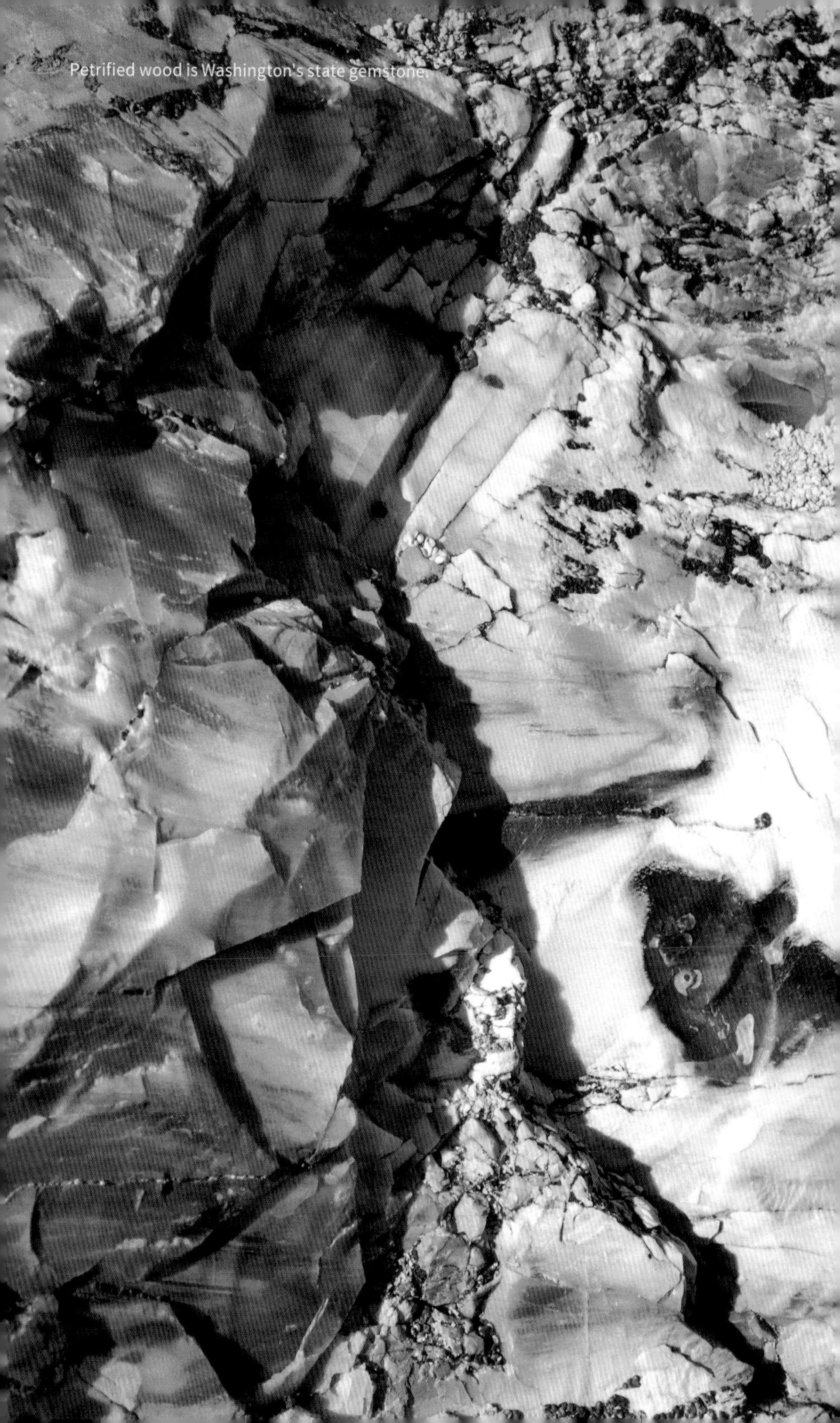

Petrified wood is Washington's state gemstone.

WASHINGTON STATE
Symbols, Emblems, and Trivia

COUNTIES: 39
POPULATION, PER THE US CENSUS: 7,535,591
FOUNDING AS US STATE: November 11, 1889 *(42nd state to enter the Union)*

STATE FLAG

As far as state flags go, Washington's is unique. Most state flags feature nods to historically important industries or landmarks, but Washington State's features something else altogether: an image of George Washington, for whom the state is named. Washington is the only state named for a US president, and it's also the only state with a president on its flag.

STATE FLOWER: Coast Rhododendron
(Rhododendron macrophyllum)

A flower of the Pacific Coast and the Cascades, the coast rhododendron isn't the showiest member of its genus, as its flowers are somewhat small, but its purple flowers are delicate and gorgeous. This species was officially named the state flower in 1959, but it has a far longer tradition as the state flower. In the run-up to the 1893 World's Fair, which was held in Chicago, Washington held a vote to determine which flower would be dubbed the state flower. The vote was only open to women and it pitted fans of clover against the coast rhododendron. The rhododendron won, but the story is also bittersweet: The election for the state flower was held well before Washington women had the right to vote in political elections. That didn't come until 1910.

STATE TREE:
Western Hemlock
(Tsuga heterophylla)

Washington State's forests are famous for towering trees. Appropriately enough, the state tree, the western hemlock, can reach an impressive 255 feet. It's not the tallest tree in the state (that honor goes to the coast Douglas-fir, which tops out at around 270 feet), but it's iconic and important as a shade tree in old-growth forests. Its sweeping branches help create the shady conditions found in the Evergreen State's understory, and its drooping top makes it easy to identify taller specimens.

STATE FISH: Steelhead Trout (*Oncorhynchus mykiss*)

The steelhead trout is the same species as the Rainbow Trout, but they have different common names because of their varying lifestyle. The rainbow trout lives in freshwater all its life; steelheads, on the other hand, travel downstream and out to sea. In general, steelheads tend to be larger and are a bit less colorful than rainbow trout. Both, of course, are popular targets for anglers, as well as excellent table fare.

STATE BIRD: Willow Goldfinch
(*Spinus tristis*)

The willow goldfinch is a subspecies of the American goldfinch. When breeding, the male is a bright yellow that's impossible to miss. The female is more of a drab brown, and so is the male outside of breeding season (summer). Happily, the goldfinch is a year-round resident in much of Washington and a welcome visitor to bird feeders, especially sock-style feeders full of thistle.

STATE GEM:
Petrified Wood

Washington is well known for its volcanoes and impressive geology, but its paleontological history is fascinating too. Washington's state gem is petrified wood, which retains the structures and texture of wood but is replaced with heavy, often beautifully colorful minerals, making it a sight to see. One of the best spots to see it in Washington is at Ginkgo Petrified Forest State Park, where visitors can hike past fossils of massive trees that date back more than 15 million years. The trees fossilized after being buried in volcanic ash; over time, water trickled in, replacing the wood with minerals that preserved the structure and appearance of the wood. More than 50 fossil species (many extinct) can be found on-site, but the most famous logs are from gingko trees, a "living fossil" that still exists today. Take note, however: Fossil collecting is not allowed at the park.

STATE FRUIT: Apple

Washington State grows more apples than any other state— by far. In fact, it grows more than half of all apples in the US, more than 130 million boxes' worth per year. Famous cultivars grown in Washington include Red Delicious, Gala, Fuji, and Grannie Smith. Most orchards are found east of the Cascades. Somewhat incredibly, every apple sold in Washington is picked by hand.

STATE INSECT:
Green Darner Dragonfly
(Anax junius)

As a group, dragonflies are fascinating, beautiful creatures, and the green darner dragonfly is more interesting than most. It starts out as a larva, but you wouldn't find it zooming around in the air: as a larva the green darner is aquatic, and the nymph (as they are known) lives in the water where they feast on tadpoles and mosquito larvae. The green darner larva is particularly well known for its odd way of getting around—it shoots water out of its rear end to zoom about. Over time, a larva molts a number of times, and it eventually emerges as a bright-green adult. Its time as an adult is limited—it'll only last for the summer—but it's an impressive sight, cruising along at up to 25 miles an hour and snatching bugs out of the sky.

STATE FOSSIL: Columbian Mammoth *(Mammuthus columbi)*

Mammoths once roamed Washington and much of North America, and their fossils have been found throughout the state. Mammoths resemble elephants (and are related to them), but were larger. Columbian mammoths were especially large, topping out at perhaps 13 feet in height and weighing more up to 10 tons. (African elephants, by contrast, are "only" up to 11 feet tall and perhaps 6 tons.) Columbian mammoths thrived during the most recent ice age, but died out around 12,000 years ago, probably due to a combination of climate change and overhunting by humans. The Mammoth was dubbed the state fossil through the efforts of elementary school students at Windsor Elementary School.

STATE AMPHIBIAN:
Pacific Tree Frog (*Pseudacris regilla*)

The Pacific tree frog's name is a bit of a misnomer. It doesn't usually live in trees, instead preferring to live on the ground or in a burrow. Found throughout much of the state, these frogs range in size from just under an inch to around two inches long. Often green in color, they have the ability to quickly adjust their skin color to blend in with their surroundings.

STATE MARINE MAMMAL: Orca

Orcas, also known as killer whales, are an icon of the region, and they're especially popular in Washington, where whale watching and orca tours are common. Orcas aren't actually whales—they belong to the dolphin family instead—like dolphins, they are famous for breaching (leaping out of the water). It's an incredible sight. Unfortunately, Washington's orca populations are currently listed as endangered, with only a few dozen individuals remaining. Efforts are now underway to identify the causes of population decline and address them.

STATE MAMMAL:
Olympic Marmot
(*Marmota olympus*)

Found only on the Olympic Peninsula, this adorable ground squirrel was once a relatively common sight in Olympic National Park, where its high-pitched whistles were a familiar part of the park. Today, its numbers are dwindling, largely due to predation from coyotes, and plans are underway to help stabilize the populations. The marmot's whistle is something of a funny sight: The marmot stands up on two legs, holds its front legs by its side, and then whistles. When it does, it looks like it's a person yelling, but the sound that comes out is a high-pitched squeak.

STATE VEGETABLE: Walla Walla Sweet Onion

Walla Walla, Washington is named for the Indigenous Walla Walla people, and today the area may be most famous for its namesake Walla Walla sweet onions. The actual plants originated on Corsica, an island in the Mediterranean, but seeds were brought to Washington by Italian immigrants toward the end of the 19th century. There, the conditions were ripe for growing onions, and they've been grown in Walla Walla ever since. The city even holds a Sweet Onion Festival each year.

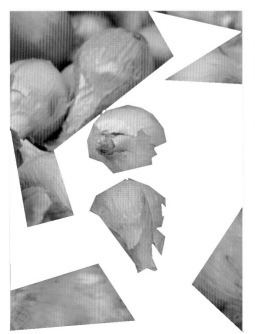

STATE SHIP: *Lady Washington* (*also see page 112*)

This replica tall ship is named after an 18th-century sailing ship of the same name; built on the East Coast, she was the first U.S. ship to arrive on the Pacific Coast, and her crew was involved in trade efforts on the coasts, as well as in Japan and elsewhere. The replica ship was built in 1989 in honor of the Washington State centennial. Harbored in Aberdeen, Washington, the ship offers ticketed sailing excursions, can be chartered, and is a common sight at festivals and events in the Pacific Northwest. You can even volunteer to serve as a crewmate! (More info: historicalseaport.org.)

STATE WATERFALL: Palouse Falls (*also see page 17*)

Located in Palouse Falls State Park in Eastern Washington, Palouse Falls tumbles 198 feet, into a massive gorge. Higher than Niagara Falls, Palouse Falls is also famous for its stunning scablands scenery. The best time to visit is when the water level is up (usually spring or summer). Incredibly—though this is not recommended—Washington kayaker Tyler Bradt kayaked over the falls, and survived to tell the tale. (Again, please do not attempt this.)

Palouse Falls

Index

About the Author

Ellie Kozlowski has lived in the Pacific Northwest for more than a decade. It is, they think, the best place to enjoy the desert, the rainforest, the ocean, and the mountains. Their book *Best Tent Camping: Washington* was released in 2018 by Menasha Ridge Press. If they're not adventuring with their partner and their dogs, they are likely in Seattle, writing poetry and working on a memoir.